Living Things in Their Environment

HOUGHTON MIFFLIN

BOSTON

Printed in the U.S.A.   ISBN-13: 978-0-547-06223-5   ISBN-10: 0-547-06223-0   4 5 6 7 8 9-0868-16 15 14 13 12 11
4500278493

Do What Scientists Do

Meet Dr. Paula Mikkelsen. She works at the American Museum of Natural History in New York City. She is in charge of the museum's collection of mollusks. The collection includes clamshells, snail shells, and the remains of slugs and squids. Dr. Mikkelsen helps other scientists find the mollusks they want to study.

Scientists ask questions. Then they answer them by investigating and experimenting.

In the Florida Keys, Dr. Mikkelsen has found 1,700 kinds of ocean mollusks. That number surprised her. It is three times the number other scientists predicted.

Dr. Mikkelsen has many questions about mollusks. For example, she wants to know how many kinds of mollusks live in the ocean around islands called the Florida Keys. To find out, she scuba dives to collect mollusks.

Back at the museum, Dr. Mikkelsen records the name of each new mollusk. Like all scientists, she keeps careful records of science information, or **data.**

Science investigations take many forms.

Dr. Mikkelsen collects animals to analyze. Other scientists make observations. Still others carry out experiments. Dr. Mikkelsen shares what she discovers with other scientists. They ask her questions about her data. Dr. Mikkelsen also shares her results with people in charge of protecting Florida wildlife. This helps them make decisions about how much scuba diving, boating, and fishing they can allow around the Keys.

Dr. Paula Mikkelsen uses tools such as these magnifying goggles to observe tiny mollusk shells.

Think Like a Scientist

The ways scientists ask and answer questions about the world around them is called **scientific inquiry.** Scientific inquiry requires certain attitudes, or ways of thinking. To think like a scientist you have to be:

- curious and ask a lot of questions.

- creative and think up new ways to do things.

- willing to listen to the ideas of others but reach your own conclusions.

- open to change what you think when your investigation results surprise you.

- willing to question what other people tell you.

What attracts the bee to the flower? Is it color, odor, or something else?

Use Critical Thinking

When you think critically you make decisions about what others tell you or what you read. Is what you heard or read fact or opinion? A *fact* can be checked to make sure it is true. An *opinion* is what you think about the facts.

Did anyone ever tell you a story that was hard to believe? When you think, "That just can't be true," you are thinking critically. Critical thinkers question what they hear or read in a book.

It looks like bees are attracted to certain flowers. I wonder if they use color, smell, or something else, to tell one flower from another?

I read that bees are attracted to flowers by their smell, but they identify different flowers by their color and shape.

Science Inquiry

Applying scientific inquiry helps you understand the world around you. Say you have decided to keep Triops, or tadpole shrimp.

Observe You watch the baby Triops swim around in their tank. You notice how they swim.

Ask a Question When you think about what you saw, heard, or read you may have questions.

Hypothesis Think about facts you already know. Do you have an idea about the answer? Write it down. That is your hypothesis.

Experiment Plan a test that will tell if the hypothesis is true or not. List the materials you will need. Write the steps you will follow. Make sure that you keep all conditions the same except the one you are testing. That condition is called the *variable.*

Conclusion Think about your results. What do they tell you? Did your results support your hypothesis or show it to be false?

Describe your experiment to others. Communicate your results and conclusion. You can use words, charts, or graphs.

My Triops Experiment

Observe Light appears to cause Triops to change how they move.

Ask a Question I wonder, do Triops like to swim more in the daytime or the nighttime?

Hypothesis If I watch the Triops in dim light and then in bright light they will move differently.

Experiment I'm going to observe how the Triops move in dim light. Then I'm going to turn on a light and observe any changes.

Conclusion When I turn on a bright light, the Triops speed up in the water. The results support my hypothesis. Triops are more active in bright light than in dim light.

Inquiry Process

Here is a process that some scientists follow to answer questions and make new discoveries.

```
Make Observations
        ↓
   Ask Questions
        ↓
    Hypothesize
        ↓
  Do an Experiment
        ↓
  Draw a Conclusion
     ↙        ↘
Hypothesis is   Hypothesis is
Supported       Not Supported
```

Science Inquiry Skills

You'll use many of these inquiry skills when you investigate and experiment.

- Ask Questions
- Observe
- Compare
- Classify
- Predict
- Measure

- Hypothesize
- Use Variables
- Experiment
- Use Models
- Communicate
- Use Numbers

- Record Data
- Analyze Data
- Infer
- Collaborate
- Research

Try It Yourself!

Experiment With a Matter Masher

To use the Matter Masher, put foam cubes or mini marshmallows in the bottle and screw on the cap. Then, push the top part of the cap up and down to pump air into the bottle.

1 Make a list of questions you have about the Matter Masher.

2 Think about how you could find out the answers.

3 Describe your experiment. If you did your experiment, what do you think the results would be?

You Can...

Be an Inventor

Jonathan Santos

His invention earned him his own trading card!

Jonathan Santos has been an inventor all his life. His first invention was a system of strings he used to switch off the lights without getting out of bed.

As a teenager, Jonathan invented a throwing toy called the J-Boom. He read about boomerangs. Then he planned his own toy with four arms instead of two. He built a sample, tried it out, and made improvements. Then he sold it in science museum gift shops.

Today, Jonathan works as a computer software engineer. He invents new ways to use computers. Jonathan is still inventing toys. His latest idea is a new kind of roller coaster!

"As a kid I quickly discovered that by using inventiveness you can design things and build things by using almost anything."

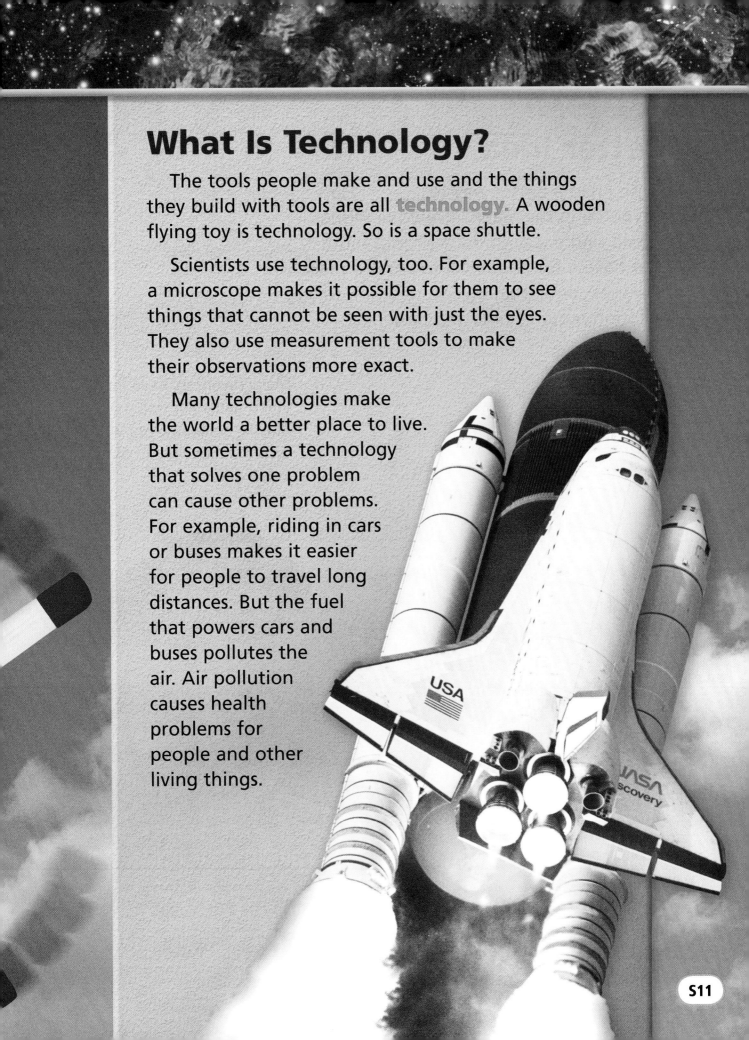

What Is Technology?

The tools people make and use and the things they build with tools are all technology. A wooden flying toy is technology. So is a space shuttle.

Scientists use technology, too. For example, a microscope makes it possible for them to see things that cannot be seen with just the eyes. They also use measurement tools to make their observations more exact.

Many technologies make the world a better place to live. But sometimes a technology that solves one problem can cause other problems. For example, riding in cars or buses makes it easier for people to travel long distances. But the fuel that powers cars and buses pollutes the air. Air pollution causes health problems for people and other living things.

USA

NASA
scovery

A Better Idea

"I wish I had a better way to _____". How would you fill in the blank? Everyone wishes they could find a way to do their jobs more easily or have more fun. Inventors try to make those wishes come true. Inventing or improving an invention requires time and patience.

Many inventors have improved video game controllers. Maybe, someday, you will invent a new way to play video games.

Video Game Controller

joystick

buttons to choose actions

direction button

How to Be an Inventor

1. **Identify a problem.** It may be a problem at school, at home, or in your community.

2. **List ways to solve the problem.** Sometimes the solution is a new tool. Other times it may be a new way of doing an old job or activity.

3. **Choose the best solution.** Decide which idea will work best. Think about which one you can carry out.

4. **Make a sample.** A sample, called a *prototype,* is the first try. Your idea may need many materials or none at all. Choose measuring tools that will help your design work better.

5. **Try out your invention.** Use your prototype or ask some else to try it. Keep a record of how it works and what problems you find.

6. **Improve your invention.** Use what you learned to make your design work better. Draw or write about the changes you made and why you made them.

7. **Share your invention.** Show your invention to others. Explain how it works. Tell how it makes an activity easier or more fun. If it did not work as well as you wanted, tell why.

You Can...

Make Decisions

Troubles for Baby Turtles

Each spring adult female sea turtles come out of the ocean in the dark of night. They crawl onto sandy beaches and dig nest holes. They lay their eggs, cover them with sand, and slip back into the ocean.

A few weeks later, and all at once, the babies hatch and climb out of the nest. Attracted to nature's bright lights, the turtles should crawl toward the lights of the night sky shining on the ocean. But on many beaches, the lights from streetlights or houses are much brighter. The baby turtles crawl away from the ocean and toward the electric lights. Instead of finding their home in the sea, many of them die.

Deciding What to Do

How could you help save the most baby turtles?

Here's how to make your decision about the baby turtles. You can use the same steps to help solve problems in your home, in your school, and in your community.

Learn → Learn about the problem. Take the time needed to get the facts. You could talk to an expert, read a science book, or explore a web site.

List → Make a list of actions you could take. Add actions other people could take.

Decide → Think about each action on your list. Decide which choice is the best one for you or your community.

Share → Communicate your decision to others.

Science Safety

☑ Know the safety rules of your school and classroom and follow them.

☑ Read and follow the safety tips in each Investigation activity.

☑ When you plan your own investigations, write down how to keep safe.

☑ Know how to clean up and put away science materials. Keep your work area clean and tell your teacher about spills right away.

☑ Know how to safely plug in electrical devices.

☑ Wear safety goggles when your teacher tells you.

☑ Unless your teacher tells you to, never put any science materials in or near your ears, eyes, or mouth.

☑ Wear gloves when handling live animals.

☑ Wash your hands when your investigation is done.

Caring for Living Things

☑ Learn how to care for the plants and animals in your classroom so that they stay healthy and safe. Learn how to hold animals carefully.

LIFE  SCIENCE

Living Things in Their Environment

Living Things in Their Environment

Independent Reading

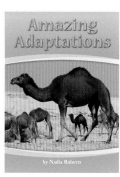

A Hungry Red Hawk

Amazing Adaptations

Forced Out

Discover!

Polar bears live on the frozen coasts of the Arctic. They hunt from the edges of ice platforms. These bears can run as fast as 40 kilometers (about 25 miles) in an hour without slipping. Why doesn't a polar bear slip on the ice when it runs? You will have the answer to this question by the end of the unit.

Chapter **4**

Survival of Living Things

Lesson Preview

LESSON 1

Water, air, a place to live—why do you need these to survive?

Read about it in Lesson 1.

LESSON 2

Bald eagles and bears both eat fish—what happens to these animals if there are not enough fish?

Read about it in Lesson 2.

LESSON 3

From the leaves of a plant to the feet of a duck—how do their parts help living things survive?

Read about it in Lesson 3.

LESSON 4

A fire spreads through a forest—can a forest fire ever be good for living things?

Read about it in Lesson 4.

What Are the Needs of Living Things?

Why It Matters...

You probably know that a turtle is alive and that a rock is not alive. But how do you know this? What does it mean to be alive? You and all other living things share some of the same traits. All living things also share the same basic needs.

PREPARE TO INVESTIGATE

Inquiry Skill

Collaborate When you collaborate, you work with others to share ideas, data, and observations.

Materials

- aquarium
- water
- gravel
- goldfish
- fish food
- piece of elodea plant

Science and Math Toolbox

For step 2, review **Making a Chart to Organize Data** on page H10.

Staying Alive
Procedure

1. **Collaborate** Work with a partner. One partner should observe a goldfish. The other partner should observe an elodea (ah LOH dee ah), which is a type of water plant.

2. **Observe** In your *Science Notebook,* make a chart like the one shown. Watch your living thing for a few minutes. In your chart, record the name of the living thing and everything you observe. Include its surroundings and any movements it makes.

3. **Infer** Based on your observations, write two or three things that you think your living thing needs to stay alive.

4. **Collaborate** Compare charts with your partner. Circle the needs that are alike for the fish and the plant.

Conclusion

1. **Compare** What does the goldfish need that the elodea plant does not need?

2. **Hypothesize** If you put the elodea plant in sunlight, it releases tiny bubbles of gas. Where do you think this gas comes from? What does the goldfish do that might be similar?

STEP 2

| Observing Living Things | |
Observations	Needs

STEP 2

STEP 4

Investigate More!

Research What animal would you like to have as a pet? Use the library to find books about what that animal needs to stay alive and healthy.

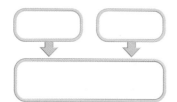
Needs of Living Things

MAIN IDEA Everything is either living or nonliving. Living things depend on both the living things and nonliving things around them to meet needs.

Living and Nonliving Things

As you look at the picture on this page, you see many things. There are flowers, bushes, sunlight, soil, a dog, and humans. Some of these things are living, and others are nonliving. A living thing is alive and is able to carry out life processes (PRAHS ehs ihz).

There are living and nonliving things in this picture. Identify as many of each kind as you can.

What are life processes? Think of the things your body does. For example, you grow and develop. You also react to the things around you. Another life process of living things is the ability to reproduce (ree pruh DOOS), or to produce young. All of these life processes use energy (EHN-ur jee). **Energy** is the ability to cause change.

Not all things are alive. A nonliving thing is not alive, so it cannot carry out life processes. What traits could you look for to decide whether something is living or nonliving? The five traits of living things are described in the table below.

▶ DRAW CONCLUSIONS   **What might happen to a living thing that doesn't get any energy?**

Traits of Living Things

Made of Cells		All living things are made of tiny parts called cells. Some living things are made up of only one cell. Humans are made of many millions of cells!
Obtain and Use Energy		Plants, such as apple trees, get energy from the Sun. Apples contain food energy. Animals obtain energy from food and use that energy to power their activities.
Respond to Surroundings		When a plant bends toward the light, it is responding to its surroundings. All living things react to changes in their surroundings.
Grow and Develop		All living things grow and develop. When you get taller, you are growing. When your body changes during your lifetime, you are developing.
Reproduce		All living things have the ability to reproduce. This means that they can produce offspring, or young that are like themselves.

Energy Leaves capture the energy in sunlight. The plant uses this energy to make food.

Needs of Living Things

You watch a bee flying just above a flower. A bee and a plant don't seem to have much in common, but both are organisms (AWR guh nihz uhmz). An **organism** is a living thing. All organisms carry out the same life processes. They also have similar basic needs. What do plants, animals, and all other organisms need to survive?

Energy Moving, growing, and breathing all require energy. All living things need a source of energy. They use food as a source of energy, but they get this food in different ways. Plants use energy from sunlight to make food. Animals cannot make food. They get energy by eating plants or other animals.

Nutrients Nutrients (NOO tree uhnts) are materials in food and soil that living things need for energy and for growth.

Air Air is a mixture of gases that living things need. One of the gases in air is oxygen (AHK sih juhn). Most living things need oxygen to survive. When plants make food they give off oxygen into the air. Animals depend on this oxygen to survive.

Nutrients Roots and stems carry nutrients and water from the soil to all parts of the plant.

Shelter All animals need a place to live. An animal's home gives it shelter and provides it with protection from enemies. Some animals use plants for shelter.

Water Living things are made mostly of water. In fact, more than three fourths of your blood is water. Most living things can live for only a short time without water.

▶ **DRAW CONCLUSIONS** Could most plants live in soil that contained no nutrients? Why or why not?

Air When you exercise, you need a lot of oxygen. Oxygen is used to break down nutrients.

Shelter Caves give bats shelter. The insects that bats eat and the water bats drink are found in or near caves.

Water The body needs water to break down food, to move things from place to place, and to make cells.

Interactions

Living things are found in every kind of environment (ehn VY ruhn muhnt). An **environment** is all the living and nonliving things that surround an organism.

A Florida mangrove swamp is one kind of ecosystem (EE koh sihs tuhm). An **ecosystem** is all the living and nonliving things that exist and interact in one place. To survive, the organisms in an ecosystem depend on each other and on the nonliving things that share their ecosystem.

▶ **DRAW CONCLUSIONS** What might happen if all of one type of organism in an ecosystem died?

Herons build nests in the leafy branches.

Mangrove trees use sunlight to make food.

Mangrove roots prevent soil from washing away.

Pelicans depend on fish for food.

Red snapper and other fish live in the water.

Oysters and crabs use mangrove roots for shelter.

Lesson Wrap-Up

Visual Summary

Living things are made up of cells, obtain and use energy, react, grow and develop, and produce offspring.

Living things need energy, nutrients, air, water, and shelter.

In an ecosystem, organisms interact with other organisms and with nonliving parts of their environment.

LINKS for Home and School

ART Design a Mural Design a mural that shows an ecosystem near your school. Include living as well as nonliving things. Try to show how the living and nonliving things interact.

LITERATURE Write a Log Entry
Imagine you are a space explorer and your ship has landed on a faraway planet. What strange life forms do you see? How can you tell if they are alive? Write a log entry that describes the life processes and environment of one life form.

Review

❶ **MAIN IDEA** What are the five traits of living things?

❷ **VOCABULARY** Write a sentence using the term *environment*.

❸ **READING SKILL: Draw Conclusions** You receive a gift that grows in sunlight and does not need to be fed. Would you conclude that this gift is a plant or an animal? Explain.

❹ **CRITICAL THINKING: Apply** Give an example of how a nonliving thing might affect the living things in a desert ecosystem.

❺ **INQUIRY SKILL: Collaborate** Name a basic need of living things. Explain to a classmate how that basic need can be met for a mouse.

✔ **TEST PREP**
Plants do, but animals do NOT ___.

A. produce offspring.

B. need water.

C. use sunlight to make food.

D. grow and develop.

 Technology
Visit **www.eduplace.com/scp/** to find out more about the needs of living things.

How Do Living Things Compete?

Why It Matters...

"It's mine!" "No, it's mine!" If birds and squirrels could speak to each other, this is what they might say. When food is limited in an environment, animals must compete. An animal that loses a competition might lose a meal or a place to live.

PREPARE TO INVESTIGATE

Inquiry Skill

Use Variables A variable is the condition that is being tested in an experiment. All conditions in an experiment must be kept the same, except for the variable.

Materials

- 4 paper plates
- 4 sheets of paper
- pretzels (1 per student)

Science and Math Toolbox

For step 5, review **Making a Bar Graph** on page H3.

Competition
Procedure

1 **Use Variables** Your teacher will set up four model ecosystems. Each ecosystem is represented by a plate covered with a sheet of paper. Some plates contain many pretzels, some contain few pretzels, and some contain no pretzels.

2 **Use Models** Stand in the center of the room. When your teacher says "Go," choose an ecosystem and walk to it. **Safety:** Do not run or push others.

3 Peek under the paper. If there is a pretzel, take the pretzel and stand by the ecosystem. If there are no pretzels, move on to another ecosystem.

4 Repeat step 3 until you find a pretzel.

5 **Communicate** When every student has found a pretzel, make a bar graph like the one shown. The graph should show how many ecosystems each student visited before finding food.

STEP 2

STEP 3

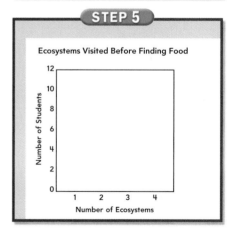
STEP 5

Ecosystems Visited Before Finding Food

Conclusion

1. **Analyze Data** How many ecosystems did most people visit before they found food? Why?

2. **Predict** How might an organism be affected if the food in its ecosystem were eaten by other organisms?

Investigate More!

Solve a Problem Take away several pretzels, then repeat the activity. Think of ways that each student could still get some food. Share your ideas with your classmates.

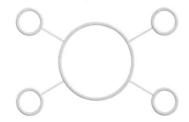
▶ **VOCABULARY**

community	p. B15
population	p. B14
resource	p. B15

▶ **READING SKILL**

Main Idea and Details
As you read, write down details that describe the ways in which organisms compete.

Living Things Compete

MAIN IDEA Organisms compete for resources when they live in the same ecosystem and have similar needs.

Competing for Food and Water

Look around. You, your classmates, your teachers, your family, and all the people who live in your neighborhood make up a population (pahp yuh LAY shuhn) of humans. A **population** is all the organisms of the same kind that live together in an ecosystem. All the ants living in a forest make up the ant population of that forest ecosystem. Every oak tree in a forest is a member of the oak tree population of that ecosystem.

coyote

snake

skunk

prairie chicken eggs

In a prairie ecosystem, coyotes, snakes, and skunks compete with each other for prairie chicken eggs.

All the populations in an ecosystem make up a community (kuh MYOO nih tee). A **community** is a group of plants and animals that live in the same area and interact with each other. The ants, oak trees, robins, and other living things in a forest ecosystem are part of the same community.

A pond ecosystem is home to animal populations such as fish, frogs, and insects. Plants such as cattails and populations of algae also live there. Living things in nature must be able to get enough resources (REE-sawrs ehz) to survive. A **resource** is a thing found in nature that is useful to organisms. Food, water, shelter, and air are resources. If there is not enough of a resource for all the organisms that need it, they must compete for the resource.

In a pond community, cattails and algae compete for nutrients in the water. Members of the same population may also compete for a resource. If there are not enough resources to meet the needs of all the organisms, some will die. For example, if there are too many frogs, some will not catch enough insects and will not survive.

above surface

below surface

▲ **Pond Community**
Competition in a community keeps populations from getting too large.

▶ **MAIN IDEA** **What are four resources for which living things compete?**

B15

Competing for Space

In addition to food and water, organisms need living space. Many birds need tree branches and holes in tree trunks to build nests. Trees need space underground for their roots to spread out. They need space above ground for their leafy branches to capture energy from sunlight.

▲ Wolf packs may move to new areas to find more space.

Wolves live in family groups called packs. Sometimes there isn't enough space for all the wolf packs in an area to live and raise offspring. Some of the packs may leave the area to find more space.

Sea lions live on rocks at the edge of the ocean. If a sea lion population in a rocky area becomes too crowded, the animals will fight for space. Some sea lions are injured or killed as a result of those fights.

Sea lions compete with one another for space. ▼

Lesson Wrap-Up

Visual Summary

All the populations that live in an area and interact make up a community.

Organisms in a region compete for resources such as food, water, air, and space.

The size of a population depends on the available resources in an area.

LINKS for Home and School

MATH **Find the Product** You are observing a frog in a pond ecosystem. You see that the frog eats 18 crickets each week. If there were 8 frogs in the pond that each ate the same amount as the first frog, how many crickets would they eat in all in one week? What problem did you solve to find the answer?

SOCIAL STUDIES **Write an Interview** Humans and animals often compete for living space and resources. Research competition between elephants and farmers in Africa. Write an interview with a farmer. Then write an interview with an elephant to show the other side of the story.

Review

❶ **MAIN IDEA** When do organisms compete for resources?

❷ **VOCABULARY** How is a population different from a community?

❸ **READING SKILL: Main Idea and Details** Explain how frogs compete for resources in a pond.

❹ **CRITICAL THINKING: Apply** How might a community of rabbits, grass, and coyotes change if most of the grass died?

❺ **INQUIRY SKILL: Use Variables** An experiment is designed to find out how the amount of food in an aquarium affects the size of the fish. What is the variable?

✓ **TEST PREP**
If a robin and a blue jay try to build their nests on the same branch, the birds are competing for ___.

A. food

B. space

C. water

D. air

 Technology
Visit **www.eduplace.com/scp/** to read more about competition.

How Do Adaptations Help Living Things?

Why It Matters...

Suppose you were an insect that lived on green leaves. What would be a good way to hide from birds that wanted to make you their dinner? Green katydids look just like the leaves they live on. All living things have special body parts or ways that they act that help them stay alive.

PREPARE TO INVESTIGATE

Inquiry Skill

Infer When you infer, you use facts you know and observations you have made to draw a conclusion.

Materials

- foods: wheat nugget cereal, shredded wheat cereal softened in water, sunflower seeds, grapes
- water bottle with water
- tools: tweezers, chopsticks, dropper, salad tongs, pliers, hand-held strainer or slotted spoon
- goggles

Science and Math Toolbox

For step 1, review **Making a Chart to Organize Data** on page H10.

Best Bird Beak

Procedure

① **Record Data** In your *Science Notebook*, make a chart like the one shown. **Safety:** Wear goggles during this activity. Do not eat any of the foods.

② **Experiment** Use each tool to pick up softened shredded wheat. Each tool represents a type of bird beak. Which tool works best? Write the name of that tool next to "softened shredded wheat" on your chart.

③ Repeat step 2 for each of the other materials. Record results in your chart.

④ The bottle of water represents a trumpet-shaped flower containing a sweet liquid called nectar. Repeat step 2 to find out which tool works best to remove water from the bottle.

⑤ **Communicate** Share your results with your classmates. Then, decide which tool you think is best for handling each material.

Conclusion

1. **Use Models** Which tool would be best for getting nectar from a flower?

2. **Infer** From your results, make an inference about how the shape of a bird's beak is related to what it eats.

STEP 1

Material	Best Tool
softened shredded wheat	
wheat nuggets	
sunflower seeds	
grapes	
water	

STEP 2

STEP 4

Investigate More!

Research Look in books, in magazines, and on the Internet for pictures of bird beaks that work like the tools in the activity. Try to find one beak for each tool. How does each bird's beak help it eat?

▶ **READING SKILL**

Problem-Solution Use the chart to identify an extreme environment. Give an example of an organism that has body structures that allow it to survive in that environment.

Problem	Solution

Adaptations Help Living Things

MAIN IDEA Body parts and behaviors are adaptations that help an organism survive.

Getting Food

Did you ever wish that you were invisible so you could take a snack without being seen? Many animals have adaptations (ad dap TAY-shuhnz) that let them become almost invisible. Then they can sneak up on food or hide from enemies. An **adaptation** is a behavior (bi HAYV-yur) or a body part that helps a living thing survive in its environment. A **behavior** is the way an animal typically acts in a certain situation.

A cat's ability to sneak up on a mouse is a behavior that is an adaptation. ▼

▲ Some spiders have body parts that they use to spin webs that trap insects.

Many types of animal behaviors are adaptations. A bee dancing to tell other bees where food can be found is an adaptation that helps that population of bees survive.

Adaptations for getting food help an organism survive. Certain adaptations let an organism get food that others can't. A hummingbird has a long, thin beak that can reach nectar deep inside a flower. The arms of sea stars have suction cups that they use to pull open the shells of clams.

Plants have adapted parts, too. Some rainforest plants have long stems that let them reach to the tops of trees. Although their roots are in the ground, their leaves are up high where sunlight can shine on them.

▲ Venus flytraps live where soil has few nutrients. They get nutrients by trapping insects.

▶ **PROBLEM AND SOLUTION** **What two kinds of adaptations help a living thing survive?**

The long-necked giraffe can eat tree leaves that are out of reach of other animals. ▶

Surviving Harsh Conditions

Living conditions in an alpine, high-mountain, ecosystem are harsh. Temperatures are low and it often snows. The land is steep and rocky. Organisms there have adaptations that help them survive.

The growing season is short. The fact that plants sprout, grow, and produce seeds quickly is an adaptation. Many plants are small. Small plants lose little water when it's windy.

Animals also have adaptations that help them survive the cold. Thick fur and layers of fat keep some animals, such as marmots and sheep, warm. Some animals sleep during very cold periods.

Some plants and animals have adaptations that are slightly better than those of others. These organisms are more likely to survive than others of their kind.

▶ **PROBLEM AND SOLUTION** **Describe an adaptation that helps an animal survive in cold temperatures.**

Needle-shaped leaves of some trees help prevent water loss.

Ptarmigans have white feathers in winter which help them blend in with the snow. In summer, their feathers are brown which helps them hide on rocky ground.

ptarmigans

Self-Defense

Most organisms have adaptations for self-defense. These are behaviors or structures that help keep an organism from being eaten by enemies. For example, when an enemy approaches, many animals will run away or hide. Some plants have spines or thorns that prevent them from being eaten. Some plants and insects contain bad-tasting chemicals. The bad taste makes them a poor choice for a meal.

Some organisms have markings, such as spots or stripes that make it hard to see them in their environment. Still other plants and animals look like other organisms that are poisonous. These harmless organisms fool their enemies into thinking they are poisonous, so they are left alone.

▶ **PROBLEM AND SOLUTION** **How does a self-defense adaptation help an organism survive?**

▲ A barrel cactus is covered with long, sharp spines, which keeps animals away.

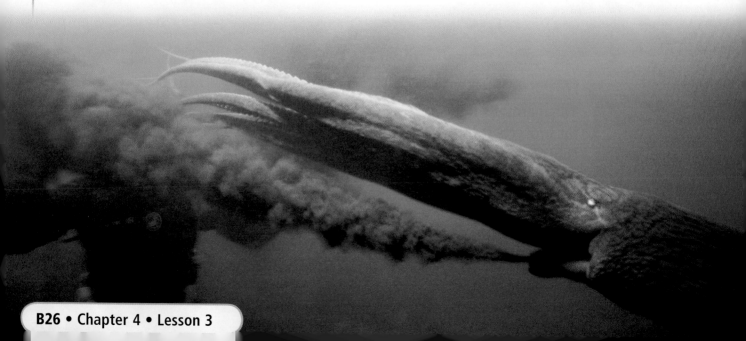

An octopus can change its color or release a cloud of ink to help it hide. ▼

Visual Summary

Adaptations help organisms:
- get food
- survive harsh conditions
- defend themselves from enemies

Body structures help organisms:
- survive
- grow
- reproduce

Behaviors help organisms:
- survive
- grow
- reproduce

LINKS for Home and School

MATH Convert Measurements Ernie is a 9,800-pound, 37-year-old Asian male elephant. Ernie is 9 feet tall and drinks 30 gallons of water each day. There are 4 quarts in a gallon. How many quarts of water does Ernie drink each day? Did you need to use all the numbers provided in this problem?

TECHNOLOGY Write a Paragraph

In nature, adaptations can take millions of years to develop. But scientists might someday discover a way to adapt an organism in a very short time. Choose an organism. How could that organism be better adapted to what it does every day? Write a paragraph to describe the adaptation and how it would help that organism.

Review

❶ MAIN IDEA Why are adaptations important?

❷ VOCABULARY Use the term *behavior* in a sentence about animal adaptations.

❸ READING SKILL: Problem-Solution How might a plant adapt to living in a desert?

❹ CRITICAL THINKING: Apply Describe an adaptation an organism might have if it lived on ice and ate animals that lived under the ice.

❺ INQUIRY SKILL: Infer What can you infer about an animal's environment if the animal has body structures that can store large amounts of water?

 TEST PREP
Which is NOT an example of self-defense?

A. An octopus squirts a cloud of ink.

B. A bee injects poison with a stinger.

C. A harmless butterfly looks like a poisonous butterfly.

D. A sea star uses its suction cups to open a clam shell.

 Technology
Visit **www.eduplace.com/scp/** to learn more about adaptations.

B27

The Wump World is a story about fictional creatures that must adapt to a changing environment. The Wumps are forced to live underground when their planet becomes polluted. Read an excerpt from The Wump World below. In Deer, Moose, Elk, and Caribou, read about how real-life animals adapt to changes in their environment.

The Wump World
by Bill Peet

... the poor Wumps remained underground wandering aimlessly through the caverns feeding on the fuzzy green moss growing on the ledges and the mushrooms clustered in the crannies, and sipping the sweet water from pools fed by underground springs. But they were very unhappy. For all they knew, they might have had to spend the rest of their days down there.

Deer, Moose, Elk, & Caribou
by Deborah Hodge

To survive, the deer family needs wild, wooded areas. When people clear land for houses and roads, wild areas get smaller. The number of cougars and wolves also shrinks. With fewer enemies, too many deer end up in one area. Food becomes scarce, and some deer die. Others eat farmers' crops to stay alive.

Sharing Ideas

1. **READING CHECK** How did the Wumps adapt when their environment became polluted?

2. **WRITE ABOUT IT** Do you think that deer are able to adapt? Give reasons for your answer. If you think deer are able to adapt, compare the way that the Wumps adapted to the way that deer adapt.

3. **TALK ABOUT IT** Tell a story about a group of fictional characters that must adapt to a changing environment.

What Happens When Habitats Change?

Why It Matters...

You may have seen headlines about an oil tanker accidentally spilling oil into water. The oil coats the fur and feathers of water animals. An animal can't keep warm with oil on its body. Oil-coated birds can't float or fly, and may drown. Organisms are affected in different ways when their environments change.

PREPARE TO INVESTIGATE

Inquiry Skill

Use Models You can use a model of an object, process, or idea to better understand or describe how it works.

Materials

- large feather
- baby oil
- balance
- water
- dropper
- disposable gloves
- aluminum pan

Science and Math Toolbox

For step 3, review **Using a Balance** on page H9.

Feather Failure

Procedure

STEP 4

1. **Communicate** Work with a partner. In your *Science Notebook*, make a two-column chart with the headings *Dry* and *Oily*.

2. **Observe** Examine a dry feather. Smooth it with your fingers. Wave it in the air. Record your observations.

STEP 5

3. **Measure** Use a balance to find the mass of the feather. Record the mass.

4. **Experiment** Smooth the feather. With a dropper, sprinkle several drops of water on the feather. Record your observations.

STEP 6

5. Put on disposable gloves. Pour baby oil into an aluminum pan. Dip the feather into the oil. Spread the oil over the entire feather.

6. Using the oily feather, repeat steps 2, 3, and 4.

Conclusion

1. **Use Models** What features of the dry feather might help a bird survive?

2. **Hypothesize** How did the oil affect the feather? How might an oil spill affect the bird population of an ecosystem?

Investigate More!

Design an Experiment Make a plan to find out how to remove the oil from bird feathers. Choose your materials and get permission from your teacher to carry out your plan. Share your results.

READING SKILL

Cause and Effect Use the diagram to show three changes in a forest habitat that are caused by a forest fire.

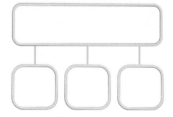

Habitats Change

MAIN IDEA Changes to an environment can have good and bad effects on the organisms that live there.

Fire and Water

How does a fire change a forest? Small plants that some animals eat are destroyed. Thick bushes that provide shelter may vanish.

But a change that is harmful to some organisms can be good for others. A fire can create new habitats (HAB ih tats). A **habitat** is a place where an organism lives.

After a flood, people and animals may lose their homes. Plants die as muddy water covers them and blocks sunlight. But when the water dries up, nutrient-rich soil is left behind. New plants can grow where they might not have grown before the flood.

Forest fires destroy habitats, but they also create conditions that allow new plants and animals to live. ▶

Plants and Animals

Living things change an environment in many ways. When beavers build a dam across a stream, the water builds up behind the dam. A pond may form. Plants or animals that lived in the once dry area may die or have to find new homes. However, new plants and animals may make the pond their habitat.

Kudzu (KUD zoo) is a fast-growing vine. It was brought to the United States from Japan. It rapidly changes the environment in which it grows. Kudzu vines grow so fast that they can cover houses and trees in a short time. The trees die because they cannot get enough sunlight.

CAUSE AND EFFECT How is a forest fire harmful to the organisms that live in a forest?

Beavers cut down trees to build dams. The areas where the trees once grew get more sunlight. ▼

Pollution

Some human activities harm the environment, and some help it. People are always building. They build houses, roads, farms, and cities. In the process, they may destroy the habitats of plants and animals.

Human activities can produce pollution (puh-LOO shuhn). **Pollution** is any harmful material in the environment. For example, chemicals that are dumped into rivers can cause fish to die. Smoke can pollute air, harming all organisms that breathe it. Garbage dumps pollute the land when harmful materials in them leak into water or soil.

It's not all bad news, though. Humans can also help the environment. People have passed laws to protect natural resources. Laws that limit hunting and fishing can help protect wildlife populations. Wildlife habitats are also protected by laws. In some places, land has been set aside for parks and wildlife reserves. And farmers plant crops in ways that keep soil healthy.

CAUSE AND EFFECT What human activities result in a better environment?

Pollution can destroy wildlife habitats. ▶

Visual Summary

Fires and floods destroy natural habitats, but they also create new ones.

Plants and animals can cause both good and bad changes in their environment.

Humans create pollution, but they also work to protect the environment.

LINKS for Home and School

MATH **Interpret Data** Around the year 1800 in England, there were about 2 dark-colored moths for every 98 light-colored moths. By 1900 there were about 95 dark-colored moths for every 5 light-colored moths. Think about how many dark- and light-colored moths there might have been in 1825, in 1850, and in 1875. Make a graph to display your guesses.

WRITING **Explanatory** Find an example of pollution in your area. Look up ways it might affect the plants, animals, and people where you live. Explain the steps that you would take to clean up or prevent the pollution. Use your ideas to write a letter to your local newspaper.

Review

❶ **MAIN IDEA** How might a change in the environment affect an organism that lives in that environment?

❷ **VOCABULARY** Define the word *habitat*.

❸ **READING SKILL:** **Cause and Effect** How can a beaver dam cause a pond to form?

❹ **CRITICAL THINKING:** **Evaluate** A forest fire can benefit living things. Give evidence to support this statement.

❺ **INQUIRY SKILL:** **Use Models** Describe a model that shows how thick vines covering a tree can cause harm to the tree.

 TEST PREP
An example of air pollution is ___.

A. smoke caused by burning a pile of old tires.

B. dumping chemicals into a river.

C. making a garbage dump.

D. destroying a habitat by building a road.

 Technology
Visit **www.eduplace.com/scp/** to find out more about changing environments.

Super Tongue

What in the world is it? It looks like a cross between a bird, a skunk, and a reptile. Meet the giant anteater of Central and South America!

At seven feet long and 80 pounds, the giant anteater is the largest anteater in the world. It may look odd, but when you get to know this creature, its unusual body parts make perfect sense.

The anteater's tongue is two feet long and is covered with tiny spines and sticky saliva to help trap ants.

A giant anteater can eat about 30,000 ants in a day!

Tail Anteaters use their long, fan-like tail to cover their head and body when resting.

Feet Huge claws help the anteater dig up the ants and termites it loves to eat. It also uses its claws to fight off enemies.

Snout Its snout is long, but its mouth is very small.

Vocabulary

Complete each sentence with a term from the list.

1. All the living and nonliving things that exist and interact in one place are a/an _____.

2. A living thing is also called a/an _____.

3. The ability to cause change is _____.

4. A behavior that helps a living thing survive is a/an _____.

5. All living things of the same kind in an ecosystem are a/an ____.

6. Something found in nature that is useful to living things and can help them meet their needs is a/an _____.

7. The way an animal acts in a situation is called a/an _____.

8. Harmful chemicals in a water supply are a kind of _____.

9. The place where a plant or animal lives is its _____.

10. Plants and animals that live in the same area and interact with each other are members of a/an _____.

adaptation B22
behavior B22
community B15
ecosystem B10
energy B7
environment B9
habitat B32
organism B8
pollution B34
population B14
resource B15

Test Prep

Write the letter of the best answer choice.

11. Which of the following is NOT a need of all living things?

    A. water
    B. energy
    C. nutrients
    D. carbon dioxide

12. Sea lions on the same crowded rock are competing for which resource?

    A. space   C. water
    B. energy   D. algae

13. An example of behavior is _____.

    A. the long neck of a giraffe.
    B. a spider spinning a web.
    C. the thick fur of a polar bear.
    D. the spines of cactus.

14. The environment of a blue whale is a/an _____.

    A. ocean   C. forest
    B. desert   D. mangrove swamp

15. Infer Suppose a population of mice and a population of owls live in a grassy meadow. Owls eat mice. About half of the mice have white fur and half have brown fur. By the end of summer, only brown mice are left. What can you infer about the overall color of the grass in the meadow? Explain how this could affect which color mice survive and which do not.

16. Use Variables A package of bean seeds says to plant the seeds 5 cm apart. You plant two groups of seeds. For one group, you plant the seeds 5 cm apart. For the other group, you plant the seeds 2 cm apart. How do you think the variable of space will affect each group? Explain.

Map the Concept

Write the terms to fill in the concept map. Organize the terms by their size relationship in the environment. The smallest unit should go in the smallest oval, the next-largest unit should go in the next-largest oval, and so on.

population   organism
ecosystem   community

1._____
2._____
3._____
4._____

Critical Thinking

17. Apply Two populations of birds live in the same habitat. Both kinds of birds eat insects. Explain how it is possible that the two populations do not compete for food.

18. Synthesize The cones of some types of pine trees release their seeds only after they have been heated to high temperatures. Explain how this adaptation improves the pine's chances of producing new trees after a forest fire.

19. Evaluate Is setting aside land for parks a good way to help the environment? Explain.

20. Analyze Imagine that you are given a fake plant and a real plant that look very similar. How can you tell which plant is real? Discuss at least three traits of living things in your answer.

Performance Assessment

Publicity Poster
Make a poster that tells other students why it is important to conserve water and land resources. How will you tell your classmates how to save resources? Display your poster at school.

Chapter 5

Food Chains

LESSON 1

From birds in the air to plants on the ground—how do living things get energy?

Read about it in Lesson 1.

LESSON 2

A frog, an insect, a leaf, the Sun—how are these things connected?

Read about it in Lesson 2.

LESSON 3

Sea stars, snails, jellies—how do these creatures depend on each other?

Read about it in Lesson 3.

How Do Living Things Get Energy?

Why It Matters...

A hummingbird flies above a flower, sipping nectar. Its wings beat so rapidly that they make a humming sound. The hummingbird needs a lot of energy to move its wings so quickly. Hummingbirds, like all living things, need energy to survive.

PREPARE TO INVESTIGATE

Inquiry Skill

Compare When you compare two things, you observe how they are different and how they are alike.

Materials

- 2 plastic cups containing soil and grass seedlings
- marking pen
- metric ruler
- aluminum foil
- plastic wrap
- plastic spoon
- water

Science and Math Toolbox

For step 2, review **Using a Tape Measure or Ruler** on page H6.

Soak Up the Sun

Procedure

1 **Collaborate** Work with a partner. Use a marking pen to label one cup of grass seedlings *Light*. Label another cup *Dark*. In your *Science Notebook*, make a chart like the one shown.

2 **Measure** Measure the height of the grass in each cup. Record the measurements on your chart.

3 Count as you add spoonfuls of water to one cup until the soil is wet. Add the same amount of water to the other cup.

4 **Use Variables** Use aluminum foil to wrap the *Dark* cup. Use plastic wrap to wrap the *Light* cup. Place both cups where they will receive indirect sunlight.

5 **Record Data** After 5 days, unwrap both cups. Observe the appearance of the grass. Then measure and record the height of the grass in each cup.

Conclusion

1. **Compare** In which cup did the height of the grass increase?

2. **Infer** Plants need energy to grow. How do you think the grass plants got the energy to grow?

STEP 1

	Height of grass (Light)	Height of grass (Dark)
Day 1		
Day 5		

STEP 2

STEP 4

Investigate More!

Design an Experiment
Does the amount of water grass gets affect how it grows? Write a hypothesis to explain what you think. Then, plan and carry out an experiment to find out. Share your results.

VOCABULARY

cell   p. B45
solar energy   p. B44

READING SKILL

Main Idea and Details
As you read, record one main idea and two details for each section.

Getting Energy

MAIN IDEA All organisms need energy to grow and survive. The Sun is the source of energy for almost all living things.

Energy from the Sun

Imagine a bright winter day. The air is cold, but your face feels warm as you tilt it toward the Sun. Sunlight feels warm on your face because light is energy. Energy is the ability to cause change.

Energy that comes from the Sun is called **solar energy**. Solar energy provides Earth with light and heat. Light and heat are energy. The Sun provides energy that plants need to make food. Most living things could not exist without solar energy.

Plants use sunlight to make food.

Plants Make Food

How does a plant get something to eat? It doesn't. Plants make food using water, air, and sunlight. The food they make is called sugar. And although plants don't "eat," they do use the food they make. Plants use the energy in the food they make to survive, to grow, and to make new plants. Dandelions use the food they make to produce new flowers. Apple trees make apples. Moss spreads and makes new plants.

Plants store some of the food they make in their cells (sehlz). A **cell** is the basic unit that makes up all living things. Plants can use this stored food when the Sun is not shining.

 **MAIN IDEA** What do plants need to make food?

Almost all energy on Earth comes from the Sun. ▼

Plants use the food they make to survive.

Animals Get Energy from Plants

Unlike plants, animals can't make food. Animals must take in food in order to get the energy that they need to survive. When an animal eats, the energy is transferred from the food source to that animal. Many animals eat plant parts. Each time an animal eats a plant, energy is transferred from the plant to that animal.

Not all of the energy that a plant gets from the Sun is transferred to an animal that eats the plant. Some energy is used by the plant for its survival. Some is stored in the plant's cells.

 **MAIN IDEA** **How do animals get energy from plants?**

A tomato plant stores energy from the Sun. Animals get some of this energy by eating the plant.

slug

human

groundhog

crow

Lesson Wrap-Up

Visual Summary

Energy from the Sun is called solar energy.

Plants use energy from the Sun to make food.

Animals that eat plants get energy from plants.

LINKS for Home and School

WRITING **Expository** People have been growing crops for thousands of years. Modern scientists use technology to improve crops. Research the history of farming. Write a paragraph about a new technology that farmers are using today.

HEALTH **Make a Chart** Nutrients are in food. Nutrients include sugar, protein, fat, vitamins, and minerals. List the main ingredients of your favorite food. Make a chart that shows each ingredient, its animal or plant source, and the nutrients it provides.

Review

1 MAIN IDEA Why do living things need energy?

2 VOCABULARY Write a sentence using the term *solar energy*.

3 READING SKILL **Main Idea and Details** List three details that support the idea that some animals get energy from plants.

4 CRITICAL THINKING: Synthesize A population of grass-eating leafhoppers live in a field. What would happen if all the grass in the field died?

5 INQUIRY SKILL: Compare How does the way plants get energy compare with the way animals get energy?

 TEST PREP
Plants survive by ___.

A. getting food from water in the soil

B. making food from water, air, and sunlight

C. getting food from the air

D. using energy from animals

 Technology
Visit **www.eduplace.com/scp/** to find out more about how living things get energy.

What Is a Food Chain?

Why It Matters...

Zip! A frog's long, sticky tongue flicks out of its mouth and captures an insect—the frog's next meal. What might the insect have eaten for its last meal? And will another living thing eat the frog? All animals must eat food, and most animals are food for others.

PREPARE TO INVESTIGATE

Inquiry Skill

Classify When you classify, you sort things into groups according to their properties.

Materials

- plant and animal picture cards
- string
- scissors
- construction-paper Sun
- transparent tape

Food-Chain Mobile
Procedure

1. **Collaborate** Work in a group. Use tape to attach a paper Sun to a string. Cut out a set of picture cards.

2. **Classify** Find the two living things that use sunlight to make food. Use string and tape to hang one of these cards from the Sun. Look at the remaining picture cards. Find the animals that eat plants. Hang one of these cards from the hanging plant card.

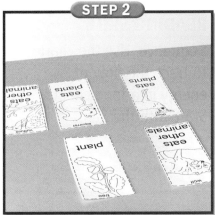

3. **Classify** Now, find the animals that eat other animals. Hang one of these cards from the hanging plant-eater card. You have made a model of a food chain. A **food chain** shows how organisms get energy.

4. **Use Models** Cut the string that connects the plant card to the plant-eater card.

5. Repeat steps 2–4 with the other cards.

Conclusion

1. **Infer** How could you organize your mobile using other card groupings?

2. **Use Models** Think about step 4. How would animals be affected if the plants they ate died out?

Investigate More!

Research Choose a plant-eating animal from your mobile. Do research to learn which plants this animal eats. Find out which animals eat this animal. Make a mobile to present to the class.

VOCABULARY

food chain	p. B50
producer	p. B51
consumer	p. B51
carnivore	p. B51
herbivore	p. B51
omnivore	p. B51

READING SKILL

Sequence Use the chart to trace the flow of energy in a food chain. Start with the Sun.

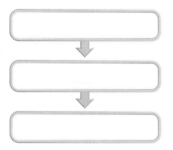

Food Chains

MAIN IDEA When one animal eats another animal or eats a plant, it becomes part of the flow of energy in a food chain.

Links in the Chain

Suppose you labeled each link of a paper chain with the name of an organism. If each organism was linked to an organism that it used for food, you would have a model of a food chain. A **food chain** is the path that energy takes through a community as one living thing eats another.

All animals depend on plants for their energy. When an insect eats a plant and then a frog eats that insect, energy is passed from organism to organism. The plant produced its own food using the energy in sunlight. Some of the Sun's energy captured by the plant passed to the insect and then to the frog.

Savanna Food Chain

Producer Savanna grass uses sunlight to make food.

Parts of a Food Chain

No matter what organisms are part of a food chain, the Sun is always the first link in the chain. Plants are the second link. A plant is called a **producer** (pruh DOO-sur) because it produces its own food.

An animal is a **consumer** (kuhn SOO mur). A consumer is an organism that eats other living things in order to get energy. Consumers are classified by their food source. An animal that eats only other animals is a **carnivore** (KAHR nuh vawr). Lions, hawks, and spiders are carnivores.

An animal such as a zebra, horse, or deer that eats only plants is an **herbivore** (HUR buh vawr). An animal that eats both plants and animals is an **omnivore** (AHM-nuh vawr). Most humans are omnivores, although some people are vegetarians. That means they don't eat meat. Producers, carnivores, herbivores, and omnivores are all parts of a food chain.

▶ **SEQUENCE** Why can't a consumer be the first link in a food chain?

Herbivore The zebra is a consumer that eats only plants.

Carnivore The lion is a consumer that eats only other animals.

Linked Food Chains

An African savanna is home to many producers and consumers. These organisms form links in different food chains. Grasses, bushes, and trees are the producers in the savanna.

Lions are carnivores. They hunt and eat zebras and gazelles.

Fire ants are omnivores that eat almost anything they can find. They eat grass seeds, small insects, and even small birds.

Ostriches are omnivores. They eat seeds, grasses, bushes, and tree leaves. Ostriches also eat small animals, such as mice.

The rhinoceros, hippopotamus, giraffe, and zebra are all herbivores. They eat only plants.

Oxpeckers are birds that are carnivores. They perch on the back of the rhinoceros and eat ticks that can harm it.

Energy from Food

How are the living things shown here linked by a flow of energy? Grass uses solar energy to make and store food in its cells. When cattle eat grass, some of the stored energy is transferred to the cells of the animal's body. Some of this energy is stored in the cells, which may eventually end up in the meatballs. When a person eats this meal, some of the energy is transferred into that person's cells.

A tomato plant also uses solar energy to make food. When people eat tomatoes, some of the energy that was stored in the tomato is transferred to them.

Spaghetti is made from wheat. Wheat plants use solar energy to make food. Humans get some of this stored energy when they eat spaghetti. Plants are always the first living link in a food chain. The person who eats a meal is the last link in the food chain.

SEQUENCE **What organisms are at the beginning of all food chains?**

The energy from the food in this meal originally came from plants.

cattle

wheat

tomato

Lesson Wrap-Up

Visual Summary

Plants are producers. Plants are the first living link in every food chain.

Herbivores eat only plants. Carnivores eat only other animals.

Animals that eat plants and also eat other animals are omnivores.

LINKS for Home and School

MATH **Multiply With 100** One 8-pound eagle must eat 8 rabbits to get enough energy to survive. Each rabbit must eat 100 pounds of grass. How many pounds of grass must be in the food chain so that one eagle can get enough energy?

LITERATURE **Write a Song or Poem** Some poems or songs repeat lines, and then add a new line at the end of each verse. One popular song of this kind is "I Knew an Old Lady Who Swallowed a Fly." Write a song or a rhyme about a food chain using this repeating style.

Review

❶ **MAIN IDEA** What is a food chain?

❷ **VOCABULARY** Write a short paragraph using the terms *producer* and *consumer*.

❸ **READING SKILL: Sequence** Describe the correct sequence of a food chain that has a carnivore, a producer, and an herbivore.

❹ **CRITICAL THINKING: Analyze** What are the relationships among a carnivore, an herbivore, and an omnivore?

❺ **INQUIRY SKILL: Classify** Suppose an animal eats only mosquitoes. Is the animal a producer or a consumer? If you classify it as a consumer, what kind of consumer is it?

✔ **TEST PREP** Which of the following is an example of an herbivore?

A. rabbit

B. lion

C. maple tree

D. hawk

 Technology Visit **www.eduplace.com/scp/** to discover more about food chains.

Exploring Underwater

In 1977, a submersible called *Alvin* allowed scientists to dive deeper than ever before. Scientists used the *Alvin* to explore the bottom of the ocean. There, they discovered many new life forms, including the giant tubeworm.

Tubeworms are worms that can be as long as 2.4 m (8 ft). They have no mouth or eyes. Until the discovery of the tubeworm, scientists believed that all food chains began with energy from the Sun. When scientists studied this amazing animal, they learned something that surprised them. Tubeworms contain bacteria that change chemicals in the water into food for the tubeworms.

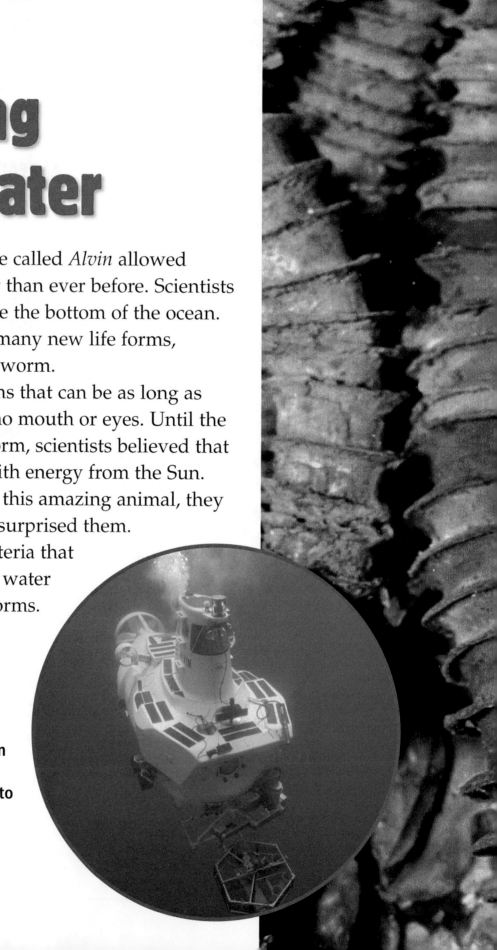

The *Alvin* was built in 1964. It was rebuilt and improved in 1977. These changes made it possible for the *Alvin* to dive to the ocean floor.

Tubeworms live thousands of meters below the surface, where sunlight cannot reach them. These giant worms live in openings in the ocean floor called hydrothermal vents. The vents shoot out water that is more than 400°C (752°F).

Sharing Ideas

1. **READING CHECK** What was the importance of the *Alvin?*

2. **WRITE ABOUT IT** Write a paragraph explaining how a food chain with a tubeworm is different from a food chain with a land animal.

3. **TALK ABOUT IT** Discuss an invention that has helped people make discoveries or learn new things.

What Are Some Different Food Chains?

Why It Matters...

Food chains exist wherever living things are found. In an ocean food chain, tiny floating plants and seaweed use solar energy to make food. The fish eat the plants and seaweed. Later, some of the fish may become a meal for a shark.

PREPARE TO INVESTIGATE

Inquiry Skill

Research When you do research, you learn more about a subject by looking in books, searching the Internet, or asking science experts.

Materials

- plant and animal picture cards

Science and Math Toolbox

For step 1, review **Making a Chart to Organize Data** on page H10.

Match Things Up

Procedure

① **Collaborate** Work in a group. In your *Science Notebook*, make a chart like the one shown.

② **Classify** Cut out a set of plant and animal picture cards provided by your teacher. Find cards that show plants and animals that live in a desert. Group these cards together. Write the names of these organisms in your chart.

③ **Research** Repeat step 2 for an ocean environment and for a rainforest environment. If necessary, use reference books or the Internet to check where an organism lives.

④ **Use Models** When all of the organisms have been classified in your chart, make a food chain for each environment. Line the cards up in order. Each food chain should start with a producer. Write or draw each food chain in your *Science Notebook*.

Conclusion

1. **Infer** What is the role of the Sun in each food chain?

2. **Communicate** Explain why you arranged each food chain the way you did.

STEP 1

Environments		
Desert	Ocean	Rainforest

STEP 2

STEP 4

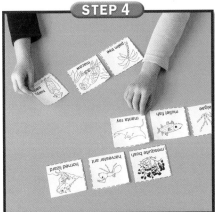

Investigate More!

Solve a Problem
Suppose you want to set up an aquarium with several kinds of fish. What would you need to know about the fish's food chains?

READING SKILL

Compare and Contrast
Use a chart to compare
and contrast food chains
in aquatic habitats and
terrestrial habitats.

Food Chains in Environments

MAIN IDEA Food chains exist wherever living
things are found. The organisms in each food chain
vary based on their environment.

Food Chains in Water

Animals live in many different places, or
habitats. Tide pools are the habitat of some
ocean animals. A tide pool is an area at the
edge of the ocean where water collects in
spaces between rocks.

A tide pool is one kind of aquatic (uh-
KWAT ihk) habitat. An **aquatic habitat** is a
place where organisms live in or on water.
In tide pools, seaweed and algae are the
producers. Like producers on land, they use
the energy from sunlight to make food.

periwinkle

Portuguese man-of-war

minnow

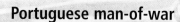

shrimp

blue crab

bladderwort
seaweed

An aquatic habitat is also home to herbivores, carnivores, and omnivores. Look at the picture of the tide pool. What food chains can you find?

▶ **COMPARE AND CONTRAST** Compare a producer that lives in an aquatic habitat with one that lives on land.

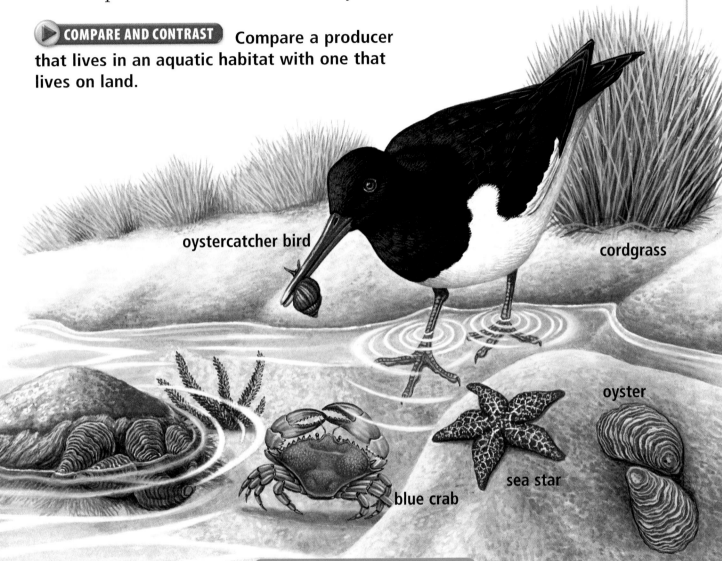

oystercatcher bird

cordgrass

oyster

sea star

blue crab

Tide Pool Food Chain

Cordgrass
This grass captures energy from the Sun to make food.

Periwinkle snail
This snail eats and scrapes plants from rocks with its mouth.

Blue crab
This crab uses its strong claws to capture and eat snails.

Food Chains on Land

People live in terrestrial (tuh REHS tree uhl) habitats. A **terrestrial habitat** is a place where organisms live on land. A desert is one kind of terrestrial habitat.

Desert regions usually get little rainfall, so they are very dry. Organisms that live in the desert are adapted to the dry conditions there. Desert producers include grasses, wildflowers, and cactuses. Cactuses store large amounts of water in their cells.

Desert herbivores include insects and small animals like rabbits. Desert herbivores that eat cactus are able to get both energy and water from the plants they eat.

prickly pear cactus

black-collared lizard

road runner

white-tailed antelope squirrel

Desert Food Chain

Evening primrose
This plant blooms at night, when desert temperatures are cool.

Antelope squirrel
This squirrel eats primrose, seeds, and small animals.

Rattlesnake
This snake eats rabbits, mice, squirrels, and birds.

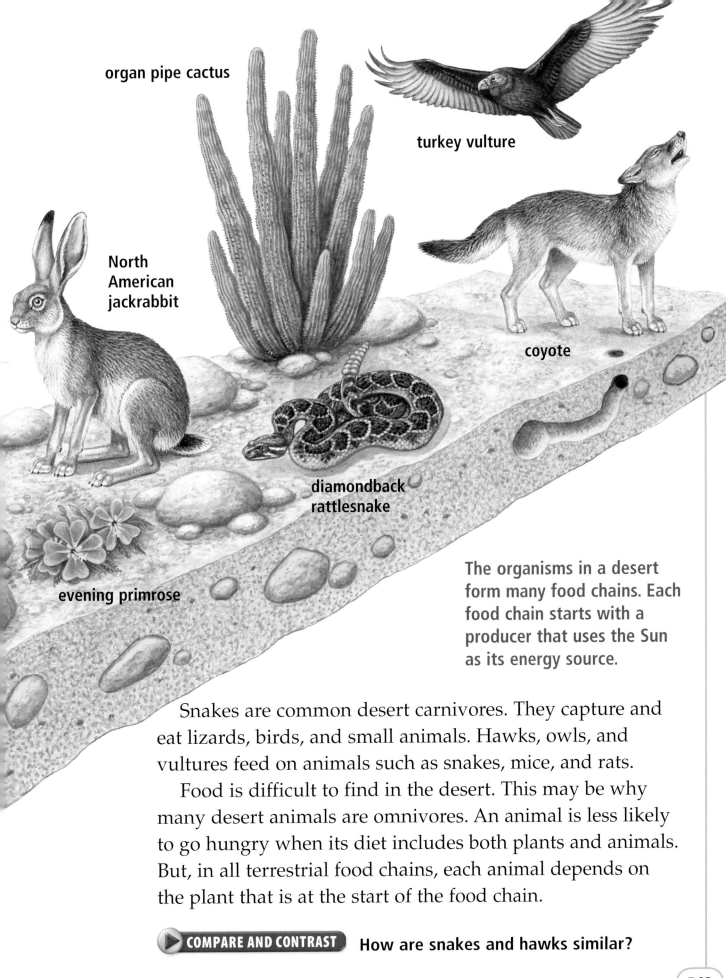

organ pipe cactus

turkey vulture

North American jackrabbit

coyote

diamondback rattlesnake

evening primrose

The organisms in a desert form many food chains. Each food chain starts with a producer that uses the Sun as its energy source.

Snakes are common desert carnivores. They capture and eat lizards, birds, and small animals. Hawks, owls, and vultures feed on animals such as snakes, mice, and rats.

Food is difficult to find in the desert. This may be why many desert animals are omnivores. An animal is less likely to go hungry when its diet includes both plants and animals. But, in all terrestrial food chains, each animal depends on the plant that is at the start of the food chain.

▶ **COMPARE AND CONTRAST**   How are snakes and hawks similar?

Visual Summary

Food chains in aquatic habitats are made up of plants and animals that live in or on water.

Food chains in terrestrial habitats are made up of plants and animals that live on land.

LINKS for Home and School

MATH Draw Lines of Symmetry Suppose that an enormous sea star has been discovered in the Pacific Ocean. Draw the sea star with five arms. Draw a line of symmetry. Suppose the sea star loses one arm, and in its place two new arms grow back. Draw the sea star with its new arms. Does it have the same line of symmetry as the first sea star you drew?

SOCIAL STUDIES Write a Journal Entry
The Inuit are a people who live near the ocean in the snowy Arctic. The Yanomano live in the hot rainforests of South America. Imagine you have traveled to visit both groups. Write a journal entry comparing the food sources of each group.

Review

❶ MAIN IDEA What do food chains in aquatic and terrestrial habitats have in common?

❷ VOCABULARY What does *terrestrial habitat* mean?

❸ READING SKILL: Compare and Contrast How are food chains in aquatic and terrestrial habitats different?

❹ CRITICAL THINKING: Apply What would happen to the number of herbivores in a food chain if most of the producers disappeared?

❺ INQUIRY SKILL: Research How could you find out what food is best to feed a pet iguana?

 TEST PREP
In an aquatic habitat, the producer in a food chain ___.

A. gets its food from water.

B. is likely to be an herbivore.

C. uses solar energy to make food for other producers.

D. uses solar energy to make its own food.

 Technology
Visit **www.eduplace.com/scp/** to find out more about terrestrial habitats.

Soil Conservationist

Soil conservationists are experts on soil. They develop ways to help farmers keep their land fertile, moist, and rich in nutrients. They also advise government agencies and businesses on how to use land without harming it.

What It Takes!

- A degree in environmental studies, forestry, or agriculture
- Investigative and research skills

Ecotourist Guide

As an ecotourist guide, you could find yourself leading safaris in Africa, exploring South American rainforests, or hiking glaciers in Alaska. Ecotourist guides take adventure-seekers on vacations to natural areas. They teach people about protecting wildlife and the environment.

What It Takes!

- A high-school diploma
- An interest in nature, ecology, and adventure

Big Mouth!

Its jaws are as long as a rowboat. The amount of food it eats each day can weigh more than a car. So this humpback whale must eat lots of really *big* fish—right?

Wrong! The humpback mainly eats krill—tiny creatures smaller than your pinky. Why? Krill are one of the most plentiful foods in the ocean. They are part of a food chain that begins with tiny ocean plants called phytoplankton. Krill eat these microscopic plants, and whales and many fish eat the krill. There are so many krill in the ocean, the humpback can eat them by the ton!

The krill is a crustacean, similar to a shrimp. It has a hard shell and no backbone.

No teeth, no problem! Instead of teeth, the humpback has baleen. These comb-like plates hang from the whale's upper jaw. The whale scoops up water in its huge mouth and squeezes it through the baleen, which traps the krill.

Vocabulary

Complete each sentence with a term from the list.

1. The path that energy takes through a community as one living thing eats another is a/an _____.

2. An animal that eats only plants is a/an _____.

3. Lions, zebras, and grass are all found in a/an _____.

4. An organism that makes its own food is a/an _____.

5. An animal that only eats animals is a/an _____.

6. Plants are able to make food by capturing ____ from the Sun.

7. An organism that eats other living things in order to get energy is a/an _____.

8. Fish and other water organisms live in a/an _____.

9. The basic unit that makes up all living things is a/an _____.

10. An animal that eats both plants and animals is a/an _____.

aquatic habitat B60
carnivore B51
cell B45
consumer B51
food chain B50
herbivore B51
omnivore B51
producer B51
solar energy B44
terrestrial habitat B62

Test Prep

Write the letter of the best answer choice.

11. Which is a terrestrial habitat?

    A. desert.
    B. river.
    C. ocean.
    D. lake.

12. In the following food chain, the producer is the _____.

    plant caterpillar bird cat

    A. bird.   C. plant.
    B. caterpillar.   D. cat.

13. In a food chain, consumers _____.

    A are usually the first link in the chain.
    B. eat other living things.
    C. use solar energy to make food.
    D. get energy from air.

14. The organism that would most likely be last in a food chain is a _____.

    A. seaweed.   C. maple tree.
    B. human.   D. caterpillar.

15. **Classify** Classify each organism in this food chain as a producer or consumer.

grass   cow   human

16. **Compare** Suppose a tree is planted in a small grassy field. As years pass, the tree grows. Over time, the grass beneath the tree dies. For what reason might the grass die? Compare the conditions for grass growing under the tree with the conditions for grass growing in the rest of the field.

Map the Concept

The chart shows two categories. Classify each organism on the list. Check that you have placed each organism in the correct category.

dandelion	crab
seaweed	grass
squirrel	zebra

Producer	Consumer

17. **Apply** A sparrow, a hawk, a rosebush, and a beetle are links in the same food chain. Put the parts of the food chain in order to trace the path of energy. What is the original source of the energy in the food chain?

18. **Synthesize** A plant on your dresser appears to be dying. Your friend suggests that you move the plant to a windowsill. What does your friend think the plant needs?

19. **Evaluate** Suppose you had to prepare a classroom display of pet animals. Your classmates have brought a turtle, a frog, a snake, and a hamster for the display. How would you decide which animals, if any, could be displayed together in the same container?

20. **Analyze** If living conditions became difficult, why might an omnivore be better able to survive than either an herbivore or a carnivore?

Performance Assessment

Plan a Dinner
Choose one of the three kinds of consumers: herbivore, omnivore, or carnivore. Plan a dinner menu for your consumer. Be creative. You might include a soup, a salad, a main course, and a dessert. Describe the ingredients in each of the menu items. Explain why your consumer would eat each menu item.

Write the letter of the best answer choice.

1. Which is NOT an example of a structure that is an adaptation?

   A. needle shaped leaves

   B. suction cups on the arm of a sea star

   C. the long, thin beak of a hummingbird

   D. a cat sneaking up on a mouse

2. Which is the source of energy for plants?

   A.

   B.

   C.

   D.

3. For which resource do squirrels and birds drinking from a birdbath compete?

   A. air

   B. food

   C. space

   D. water

4. Which organism in this food chain is an herbivore?

   A. coyote

   B. day lily

   C. rat

   D. snail

5. BOTH plants and animals _____.

   A. reproduce.

   B. give off oxygen.

   C. look for a home.

   D. use sunlight directly for energy.

6. Which is MOST likely to be an adaptation for self-defense?

   A. the thick fur coat of a bear

   B. a thick plant stem that stores water

   C. the webbed feet of a bird that lives in water

   D. a rabbit that has brown fur in summer and white fur in winter

7. Which is NOT an adaptation of a living thing to its environment?

    A. the very sharp claws of a cat

    B. the thick winter coat of a rabbit

    C. the spines that cover a desert cactus

    D. the very long stem of a rainforest plant

8. Which organism could be a consumer in an aquatic habitat?

A.

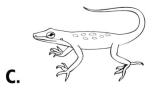

B.

C.

D.

Answer the following in complete sentences.

9. Beavers build a dam across a stream. Which is likely to benefit MORE from the dam—the fish in the stream or the trees along the stream? Explain your answer.

10. The following organisms live in a desert habitat.

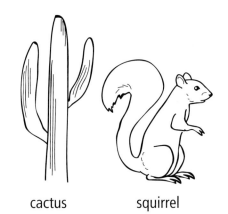

cactus   squirrel

rabbit   rattlesnake

Which two organisms are most likely to compete for food? Explain why you made your choice.

Wrap-Up

Discover!

Polar bears are adapted to the cold, icy environment of the Arctic. Thick fur and a layer of fat keep them warm in freezing temperatures. Even their paws are adapted for their environment. These adaptations make it easy for polar bears to walk on ice without slipping.

Polar bears have four paws that can be over 25 cm (about 10 in.) wide. Each paw has five toes, and each toe has a long sharp claw. These claws help polar bears grip the ice.

Each polar bear paw has seven footpads. The footpads are made of a thick, black layer of skin and are covered with small bumps. The bumps on the bear's footpads are like the treads on a sport shoe. They grip the ice and keep the bear from slipping when it runs.

Long fur between the footpads and toes keeps polar bears from slipping, too. Webbing that is under the fur between the toes helps polar bears swim.

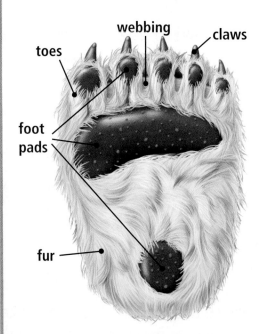

toes webbing claws foot pads fur

Learn more about animal adaptations. Go to **www.eduplace.com/scp/** to see how polar bears and other animals adapt to their environments.

Science and Math Toolbox

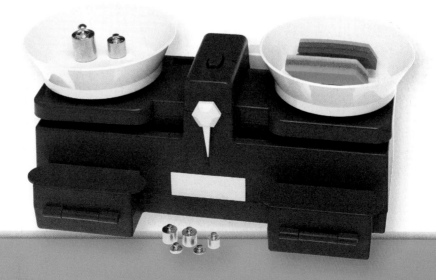

Using a Hand Lens

A hand lens is a tool that magnifies objects, or makes objects appear larger. This makes it possible for you to see details of an object that would be hard to see without the hand lens.

Look at a Coin or a Stamp

1. Place an object such as a coin or a stamp on a table or other flat surface.

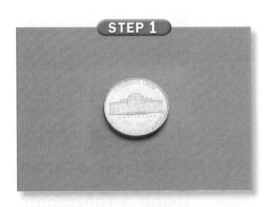
STEP 1

2. Hold the hand lens just above the object. As you look through the lens, slowly move the lens away from the object. Notice that the object appears to get larger and a little blurry.

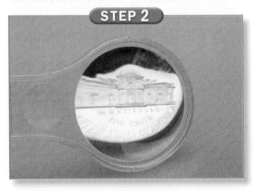
STEP 2

3. Move the hand lens a little closer to the object until the object is once again in sharp focus.

STEP 3

Making a Bar Graph

A bar graph helps you organize and compare data.

Make a Bar Graph of Animal Heights

Animals come in all different shapes and sizes. You can use the information in this table to make a bar graph of animal heights.

1. Draw the side and the bottom of the graph. Label the side of the graph as shown. The numbers will show the height of the animals in centimeters.

2. Label the bottom of the graph. Write the names of the animals at the bottom so that there is room to draw the bars.

3. Choose a title for your graph. Your title should describe the subject of the graph.

4. Draw bars to show the height of each animal. Some heights are between two numbers.

Heights of Animals

Animal	Height (cm)
Bear	240
Elephant	315
Cow	150
Giraffe	570
Camel	210
Horse	165

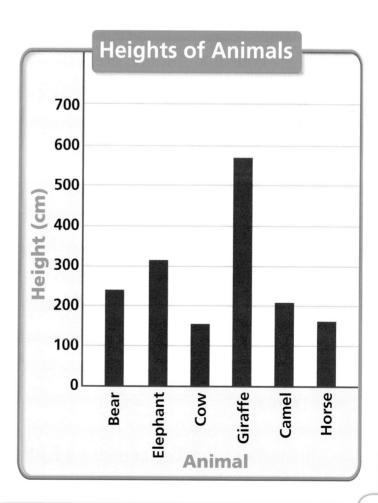

Heights of Animals

Using a Calculator

After you've made measurements, a calculator can help you analyze your data.

Add and Multiply Decimals

Suppose you're an astronaut. You may take 8 pounds of Moon rocks back to Earth. Can you take all the rocks in the table? Use a calculator to find out.

Weight of Moon Rocks	
Moon Rock	**Weight of Rock on Moon (lb)**
Rock 1	1.7
Rock 2	1.8
Rock 3	2.6
Rock 4	1.5

1️⃣ To add, press:

[1] [.] [7] [+] [1] [.] [8] [+]
[2] [.] [6] [+] [1] [.] [5] [=]

Display: [7.6]

2️⃣ If you make a mistake, press the left arrow key and then the Clear key. Enter the number again. Then continue adding.

3️⃣ Your total is 7.6 pounds. You can take the four Moon rocks back to Earth.

4️⃣ How much do the Moon rocks weigh on Earth? Objects weigh six times as much on Earth as they do on the Moon. You can use a calculator to multiply.

Press: [7] [.] [6] [×] [6] [=]

Display: [45.6]

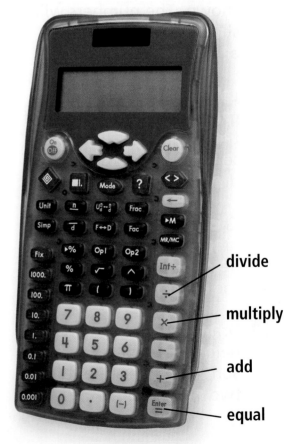

divide

multiply

add

equal

The rocks weigh 45.6 pounds on Earth.

Making a Tally Chart

A tally chart can help you keep track of items you are counting. Sometimes you need to count many different items. It may be hard to count all of the items of the same type as a group. That's when a tally chart can be helpful.

Make a Tally Chart of Birds Seen

A group of bird watchers made a tally chart to record how many birds of each type they saw. Here are the tallies they have made so far.

- Every time you count one item, make one tally.

- When you reach five, draw the fifth tally as a line through the other four.

- To find the total number of robins, count by fives and then ones.

- You can use the tally chart to make a chart with numbers.

Birds Seen

Type of Bird	Tally
Cardinal	||
Blue jay	⊬⊬⊬ ⊬⊬⊬ ⊬⊬⊬
Mockingbird	||||
Hummingbird	⊬⊬⊬ ||
House sparrow	⊬⊬⊬ ⊬⊬⊬ ⊬⊬⊬ ⊬⊬⊬	
Robin	⊬⊬⊬ ⊬⊬⊬ ||

What kind of bird was seen most often?

- Now use a tally chart to record how many cars of different colors pass your school.

Birds Seen

Type of Bird	Number
Cardinal	2
Blue jay	15
Mockingbird	4
Hummingbird	7
House sparrow	21
Robin	12

Using a Tape Measure or Ruler

Tape measures and rulers are tools for measuring the length of objects and distances. Scientists most often use units such as meters, centimeters, and millimeters when making length measurements.

Use a Tape Measure

1. Measure the distance around a jar. Wrap the tape around the jar.

2. Find the line where the tape begins to wrap over itself.

3. Record the distance around the jar to the nearest centimeter.

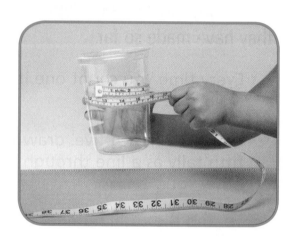

Use a Metric Ruler

1. Measure the length of your shoe. Place the ruler or the meterstick on the floor. Line up the end of the ruler with the heel of your shoe.

2. Notice where the other end of your shoe lines up with the ruler.

3. Look at the scale on the ruler. Record the length of your shoe to the nearest centimeter and to the nearest millimeter.

Measuring Volume

A beaker, a measuring cup, and a graduated cylinder are used to measure volume. Volume is the amount of space something takes up. Most of the containers that scientists use to measure volume have a scale marked in milliliters (mL).

Beaker
50 mL

Measuring cup
50 mL

Graduated cylinder
50 mL

Measure the Volume of a Liquid

1. Measure the volume of juice. Pour some juice into a measuring container.

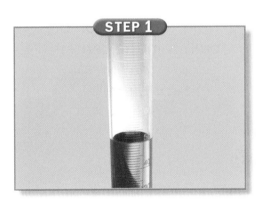

STEP 1

2. Move your head so that your eyes are level with the top of the juice. Read the scale line that is closest to the surface of the juice. If the surface of the juice is curved up on the sides, look at the lowest point of the curve.

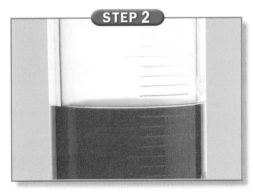

STEP 2

3. Read the measurement on the scale. You can estimate the value between two lines on the scale.

Using a Thermometer

A thermometer is used to measure temperature. When the liquid in the tube of a thermometer gets warmer, it expands and moves farther up the tube. Different scales can be used to measure temperature, but scientists usually use the Celsius scale.

Measure the Temperature of a Liquid

1. Half fill a cup with warm tap water.

2. Hold the thermometer so that the bulb is in the center of the liquid. Be sure that there are no bright lights or direct sunlight shining on the bulb.

3. Wait a few minutes until you see the liquid in the tube of the thermometer stop moving. Read the scale line that is closest to the top of the liquid in the tube. The thermometer shown reads 22°C (72°F).

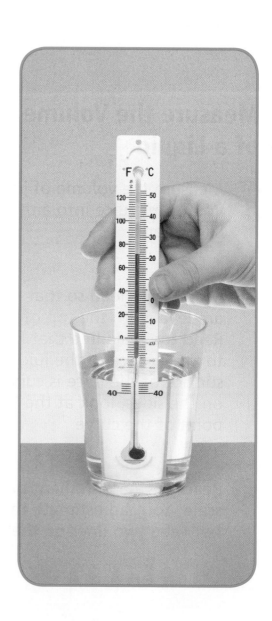

Using a Balance

A balance is used to measure mass. Mass is the amount of matter in an object. To find the mass of an object, place it in the left pan of the balance. Place standard masses in the right pan.

Measure the Mass of a Ball

1 Check that the empty pans are balanced, or level with each other. When balanced, the pointer on the base should be at the middle mark. If it needs to be adjusted, move the slider on the back of the balance a little to the left or right.

2 Place a ball on the left pan. Then add standard masses, one at a time, to the right pan. When the pointer is at the middle mark again, each pan holds the same amount of matter and has the same mass.

3 Add the numbers marked on the masses in the pan. The total is the mass of the ball in grams.

Making a Chart to Organize Data

A chart can help you keep track of information. When you organize information, or data, it is easier to read, compare, or classify it.

Classifying Animals

Suppose you want to organize this data about animal characteristics. You could base the chart on the two characteristics listed—the number of wings and the number of legs.

1. Give the chart a title that describes the data in it.

2. Name categories, or groups, that describe the data you have collected.

3. Make sure the information is recorded correctly in each column.

Next, you could make another chart to show animal classification based on number of legs only.

My Data

Fleas have no wings. Fleas have six legs.

Snakes have no wings or legs.

A bee has four wings. It has six legs.

Spiders never have wings. They have eight legs.

A dog has no wings. It has four legs.

Birds have two wings and two legs.

A cow has no wings. It has four legs.

A butterfly has four wings. It has six legs.

Animals–Number of Wings and Legs

Animal	Number of Wings	Number of Legs
Flea	0	6
Snake	0	0
Bee	4	6
Spider	0	8
Dog	0	4
Bird	2	2
Butterfly	4	6

Reading a Circle Graph

A circle graph shows a whole divided into parts. You can use a circle graph to compare the parts to each other. You can also use it to compare the parts to the whole.

A Circle Graph of Fuel Use

This circle graph shows fuel use in the United States. The graph has 10 equal parts, or sections. Each section equals $\frac{1}{10}$ of the whole. One whole equals $\frac{10}{10}$.

Oil Of all the fuel used in the United States, 4 out of 10 parts, or $\frac{4}{10}$, is oil.

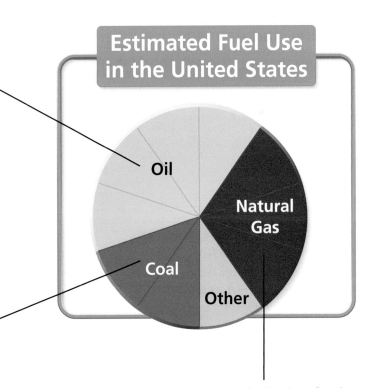

Estimated Fuel Use in the United States

Coal Of all the fuel used in the United States, 2 out of 10 parts, or $\frac{2}{10}$, is coal.

Natural Gas Of all the fuel used in the United States, 3 out of 10 parts, or $\frac{3}{10}$, is natural gas.

Measuring Elapsed Time

A calendar can help you find out how much time has passed, or elapsed, in days or weeks. A clock can help you see how much time has elapsed in hours and minutes. A clock with a second hand or a stopwatch can help you find out how many seconds have elapsed.

Using a Calendar to Find Elapsed Days

This is a calendar for the month of October. October has 31 days. Suppose it is October 22 and you begin an experiment. You need to check the experiment two days from the start date and one week from the start date. That means you would check it on Wednesday, October 24, and again on Monday, October 29. October 29 is 7 days after October 22.

Days of the Week
Monday, Tuesday, Wednesday, Thursday, and Friday are weekdays. Saturday and Sunday are weekends.

Last Month
Last month ended on Sunday, September 30.

October

Sunday	Monday	Tuesday	Wednesday	Thursday	Friday	Saturday
	1	2	3	4	5	6
7	8	9	10	11	12	13
14	15	16	17	18	19	20
21	22	23	24	25	26	27
28	29	30	31			

Next Month
Next month begins on Thursday, November 1.

Using a Clock or a Stopwatch to Find Elapsed Time

You need to time an experiment for 20 minutes.

It is 1:30 P.M.

Stop at 1:50 P.M.

You need to time an experiment for 15 seconds. You can use the second hand of a clock or watch.

Start the experiment when the second hand is on number 6.

Stop when 15 seconds have passed and the second hand is on the 9.

You can use a stopwatch to time 15 seconds.

Press the reset button on a stopwatch so that you see 0:00₀₀.

Press the start button. When you see 0:15₀₀, press the stop button.

Measurements

Volume

1 L of sports drink is a little more than 1 qt.

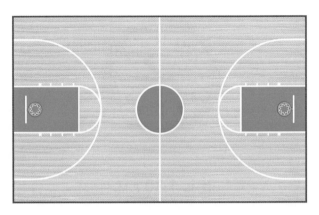

Area

A basketball court covers about 4,700 ft². It covers about 435 m².

Metric Measures

Temperature

- Ice melts at 0 degrees Celsius (°C)
- Water freezes at 0°C
- Water boils at 100°C

Length and Distance

- 1,000 meters (m) = 1 kilometer (km)
- 100 centimeters (cm) = 1 m
- 10 millimeters (mm) = 1 cm

Force

- 1 newton (N) =
  1 kilogram × 1(meter/second)
  per second

Volume

- 1 cubic meter (m³) = 1 m × 1 m × 1 m
- 1 cubic centimeter (cm³) =
  1 cm × 1 cm × 1 cm
- 1 liter (L) = 1,000 milliliters (mL)
- 1 cm³ = 1 mL

Area

- 1 square kilometer (km²) =
  1 km × 1 km
- 1 hectare = 10,000 m²

Mass

- 1,000 grams (g) = 1 kilogram (kg)
- 1,000 milligrams (mg) = 1 g

Temperature

The temperature at an indoor basketball game might be 27°C, which is 80°F.

Length and Distance

A basketball rim is about 10 ft high, or a little more than 3 m from the floor.

Customary Measures

Temperature

- Ice melts at 32 degrees Fahrenheit (°F)
- Water freezes at 32°F
- Water boils at 212°F

Length and Distance

- 12 inches (in.) = 1 foot (ft)
- 3 ft = 1 yard (yd)
- 5,280 ft = 1 mile (mi)

Weight

- 16 ounces (oz) = 1 pound (lb)
- 2,000 pounds = 1 ton (T)

Volume of Fluids

- 8 fluid ounces (fl oz) = 1 cup (c)
- 2 c = 1 pint (pt)
- 2 pt = 1 quart (qt)
- 4 qt = 1 gallon (gal)

Metric and Customary Rates

km/h = kilometers per hour

m/s = meters per second

mph = miles per hour

Health and Fitness Handbook

Health means more than just not being ill. There are many parts to health. Here are some questions you will be able to answer after reading this handbook.

- How do my body systems work?
- What nutrients does my body need?
- How does being active help my body?
- How can I be safe at home?
- How can I prevent food from making me ill?

The Digestive System

Your digestive system breaks down food into materials your body can use. These materials are called nutrients.

1 Digestion starts in your mouth.
- Your teeth break food into small pieces. Saliva mixes with the food. Saliva has chemicals that break down food more.
- Your tongue pushes the chewed food into your esophagus when you swallow.

2 Food travels through the esophagus to the stomach.
- Acid and other chemicals in the stomach break down the food even more.
- The food moves to the small intestine.

3 More chemicals flow into the small intestine. They come from the liver, pancreas, and other organs.
- These chemicals finish breaking down the food into nutrients.
- The nutrients are absorbed into the blood.
- The blood carries the nutrients to all parts of the body.

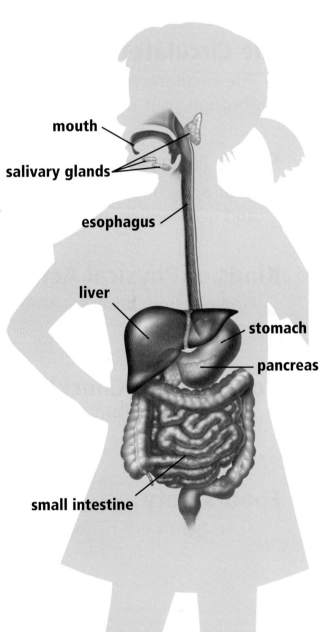

mouth

salivary glands

esophagus

liver

stomach

pancreas

small intestine

The Circulatory System

Your circulatory system moves blood through your body. There are three major parts to the circulatory system: the heart, blood vessels, and blood.

Heart Your heart has four chambers, or sections.

- The right two chambers take blood from the body and pump it to the lungs.
- There, the blood picks up oxygen and gets rid of waste.
- The left two chambers take blood from the lungs and pump it to the rest of the body.

Blood Vessels Two kinds of vessels carry blood through your body.

- **Arteries** carry blood from the heart to the body.
- **Veins** carry blood from the body to the heart.

Blood Your blood carries oxygen from your lungs to your body cells.

- Blood carries nutrients from your digestive system.
- Blood carries wastes away from the cells to organs that remove the wastes from the body.

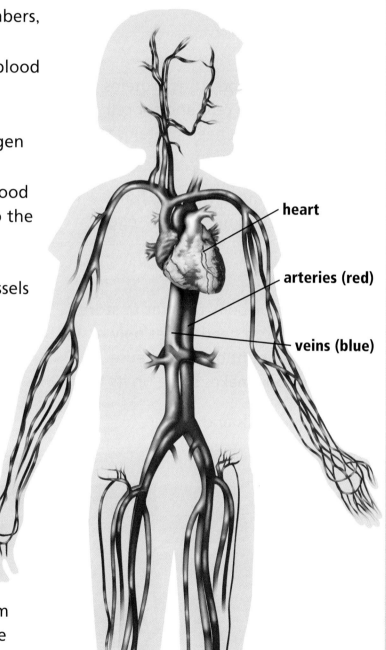

heart

arteries (red)

veins (blue)

Some Nutrients You Need

Nutrients are materials your body needs for energy and to grow. Three important nutrients are proteins, carbohydrates, and fats. Eating these nutrients in the right amount can help you stay at a healthful weight.

Proteins

Uses Your body uses proteins to build new cells and for cell activities. You need proteins to grow and develop.

Sources meat, chicken, fish, milk, cheese, nuts, beans, eggs

Fats

Uses Your body uses fat to store energy. You need to eat only a small amount of fat, because your body makes some on its own.

Sources oils and butter

Carbohydrates

Uses Carbohydrates are your body's main source of energy. Simple carbohydrates give quick energy. Complex carbohydrates give long-lasting energy. Complex carbohydrates should make up the largest part of your diet.

Sources simple carbohydrates: fruits and milk products

complex carbohydrates: whole-grain bread, cereal, pasta, potatoes

carbohydrate fat protein

Kinds of Physical Activity

Do you run, jump, and play every day? There are different kinds of physical activity. Each helps your body in a different way.

Endurance

Some activities help your body work hard for longer periods of time.

Activities That Build Endurance

- swimming
- jumping rope
- soccer
- in-line skating
- riding a bike
- walking fast
- basketball
- hockey

Do one of these activities for 20 to 60 minutes three to five times a week.

Flexibility

Stretching helps your muscles move smoothly.

Activities That Build Flexibility

- touching your toes
- stretching your arms
- sit and reach
- stretching your side

Do flexibility exercises two to three times a week.

Strength

These exercises make your muscles stronger. Ask an adult to show you how to do them safely.

Activities That Build Strength

- sit-ups
- push-ups
- pull-ups

Do strength training two to three days each week.

Home Safety Checklists

Most accidents happen at home. Here are some tips for staying safe.

Fire Safety

✔ Have smoke detectors. Check the batteries twice each year.

✔ Don't play with matches or candles.

✔ Only use the stove or oven if an adult is there.

✔ Have a family fire plan. Practice your plan.

Poison Safety

✔ Some chemicals and cleaners are poisons. So are some medicines. Keep them in high places away from small children.

✔ Post the phone number for Poison Control by the phone.

Kitchen Safety

✔ Never leave the kitchen while cooking.

✔ Store knives out of the reach of children.

✔ Wipe up spills immediately. Keep the floor clear of clutter.

Electrical Safety

✔ Keep electrical cords out of areas where someone could trip on them.

✔ Don't use electrical appliances near water.

✔ Unplug small appliances when you are not using them.

✔ Make sure electric cords are not damaged. They could start a fire.

Food Safety

Foods and drinks can carry germs. These germs can cause disease. Remember these four steps to keep food safe.

Clean

✔ Wash your hands before and after you cook. Wash them again if you handle raw meat, poultry, or fish.

✔ Wash all the dishes and utensils you use.

✔ Wash your hands before you eat.

Separate

✔ Keep raw meat, poultry, and fish away from other foods.

✔ Keep cooked food away from raw food.

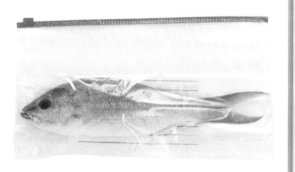

Chill

✔ Some foods need to be kept cold. Put leftovers in the refrigerator as soon as possible. This slows down the growth of germs.

✔ If you are having a picnic, keep foods in an icechest until you are ready to cook or serve them

Cook

✔ Cook food thoroughly. Cooking kills many germs.

✔ Use a thermometer to make sure foods are hot enough.

A

adaptation (ad ap TAY shuhn) A behavior or a body part that helps a living thing survive in its environment. (B22)

alloy (AL oy) A solid solution made of at least one metal. (E55)

alternate energy resource (AWL tur niht EHN ur jee REE sawrs) An energy resource other than a fossil fuel. (C52)

amphibian (am FIHB ee uhn) A vertebrate that starts life in the water and then lives on land as an adult. (A40)

analyze data (AN uh lyz DAY tuh) To look for patterns in collected information that lead to making logical inferences, predictions, and hypotheses.

aquatic habitat (uh KWAT ihk HAB ih tat) A place where organisms live in or on water. (B60)

arthropod (AHR thruh pahd) An invertebrate that has jointed legs, a body with two or more sections, and a hard outer covering. (A48)

ask questions (ask KWEHS chuhz) To state orally or in writing questions to find out how or why something happens, which can lead to scientific investigations or research.

asteroid (AS tuh royd) A piece of rock that orbits the Sun. (D48)

atmosphere (AT muh sfihr) The layers of air that cover Earth's surface. (D14)

axis (AK sihs) An imaginary line through the center of an object. (D68)

B

backbone (BAK bohn) A series of bones that runs down the back of a vertebrate animal. (A36)

behavior (bih HAYV yur) The way that an organism typically acts in a certain situation. (B22)

bird (burd) A vertebrate that has feathers, lungs, wings, and two legs and lays eggs that have hard shells. (A38)

C

carnivore (KAHR nuh vawr) An animal that eats only other animals. (B51)

cell (sehl) The smallest and most basic unit of a living thing. (A8, B45)

chemical change (KEHM ih kuhl chaynj) A change in matter in which one or more new kinds of matter form. (E23)

chemical property (KEHM ih kuhl PRAHP ur tee) A property that describes how matter can react with other kinds of matter. (E22)

chrysalis (KRIHS uh lihs) The hard case an insect forms to protect itself during the pupa stage. (A76)

classify (KLAS uh fy) To sort objects into groups according to their properties or order objects according to a pattern.

climate (KLY miht) The average weather conditions in an area over a long period of time. (D25)

collaborate (kuh LAB uh rayt) To work as a team with others to collect and share data, observations, findings, and ideas.

communicate (kah MYOO nuh kayt) To explain procedures or share information, data, or findings with others through written or spoken words, actions, graphs, charts, tables, diagrams, or sketches.

community (kuh MYOO nih tee) A group of plants and animals that live in the same area and interact with each other. (B15)

compare (kuhm PAIR) To observe and tell how objects or events are alike or different.

condensation (kahn dehn SAY shuhn) The change of state from gas to liquid. (D7)

condense (kuhn DEHNS) To change state from gas to liquid. (E15)

conifer (KAHN uh fur) A plant that makes seeds inside cones. (A72)

conservation (kahn suhr VAY shuhn) The safe-keeping and wise use of natural resources. (C62)

constellation (kahn stuh LAY shuhn) A group of stars that forms a pattern shaped like an animal, person, or object. (D86)

consumer (kuhn SOO mur) An organism that gets energy by eating other living things. (B51)

core (kohr) The innermost layer of Earth. (C14)

crater (KRAY tur) A bowl-shaped dent caused when an object from space strikes the surface of a planet or a moon. (D78)

crest (krehst) The highest point of a wave. (F15)

crust (kruhst) The thin, outermost layer of Earth. (C14)

data (DAY tuh) Information collected and analyzed in scientific investigations. (S3)

direction (di REHK shuhn) The path an object follows. (F83)

dissolve (dih ZAHLV) To mix completely with another substance to form a solution. (E52)

distance (DIHS tuhns) A measure of length. (F82)

earthquake (URTH kwayk) A sudden movement of large sections of Earth's crust. (C21)

ecosystem (EE koh SIHS tuhm) All of the living and nonliving things that exist and interact in one place. (B10)

electric circuit (ih LEHK trihk SUR kiht) A path around which electric current can flow. (F29)

electric current (ih LEHK trihk KUR uhnt) The flow of charged particles. (F28)

endangered species (ehn DAYN jurd SPEE sheez) A species that has so few members that it may soon become extinct. (A60)

energy (EHN ur jee) The ability to cause change. (B7)

environment (ehn VY ruhn muhnt) All the living and nonliving things that surround and affect an organism. (A24, B10)

equator (ih KWAY tuhr) An imaginary line around the Earth, halfway between the North Pole and the South Pole. (D26)

erosion (ih ROH zhuhn) The process of carrying weathered rock from one place to another. (C31)

evaporate (ih VAP uh rayt) To change state slowly from liquid to gas. (E15)

evaporation (ih vap uh RAY shuhn) The change of state from liquid to gas. (D7)

experiment (ihks SPEHR uh muhnt) To investigate and collect data that either supports a hypothesis or shows that it is false while controlling variables and changing only one part of an experimental setup at a time.

extinct species (ihk STIHNGKT SPEE sheez) A species that has disappeared. (A57)

filter (FIHL tur) A device or material that traps some substances and allows others to pass through. (E44)

fish (fihsh) A vertebrate that lives in water and uses gills to take oxygen from water. (A39)

food chain (food chayn) The path that energy takes through a community as one living thing eats another. (B50)

force (fawrs) A push or a pull. (F73)

fossil (FAHS uhl) The very old remains of a plant or animal. (A56, C22)

fossil fuel (FAHS uhl FYOO uhl) A fuel that forms over a very long time from the remains of plants and animals. (C50)

freeze (freez) To change state from liquid to solid. (E15)

friction (FRIHK shuhn) A force that occurs when one object rubs against another object. (F45)

fruit (froot) The part of a plant that contains the seeds. (A70)

full moon (ful moon) The phase of the Moon when all of the Moon's sunlit side faces Earth. (D75)

gas (gas) Matter that has no definite shape and does not take up a definite amount of space. (E7)

geothermal energy (jee oh THUR muhl EHN ur jee) Heat from inside Earth. (C52)

gravity (GRAV ih tee) A force that pulls objects toward each other. (F74)

habitat (HAB ih tat) The place where an organism lives. (A57, B32)

heat (heet) The flow of thermal energy from warmer objects to cooler objects. (F42)

herbivore (HUR buh vawr) An animal that eats only plants. (B51)

humus (HYOO muhs) The decayed remains of plants and animals. (C32)

hydroelectric energy (hy droh ih LEHK trihk EHN ur jee) Electricity made from the force of moving water. (C52)

hypothesize (hy PAHTH uh syz) To make an educated guess about why something happens.

igneous rock (IHG nee uhs rahk) Rock that forms when melted rock from inside Earth cools and hardens. (C18)

inclined plane (ihn KLYND playn) A simple machine made up of a slanted surface. (F94)

individual (ihn duh VIHJ oo uhl) A single member of a species. (A86)

infer (ihn FUR) To use facts and data you know and observations you have made to draw a conclusion about a specific event based on observations and data. To construct a reasonable explanation.

inner planets (IHN ur PLAN ihts) The four planets closest to the Sun: Mercury, Venus, Earth, and Mars. (D46)

invertebrate (ihn VUR tuh briht) An animal that does not have a backbone. (A46)

kinetic energy (kuh NET ihk EHN ur jee) Energy of motion. (F8)

landform (LAND fawrm) A part of Earth's surface that has a certain shape and is formed naturally. (C8)

larva (LAHR vuh) The second, worm-like stage in an insect's life cycle. (A76)

latitude (LAT ih tood) The distance north or south of the equator. (D26)

leaf (leef) The part of a plant that collects sunlight and gases from the air and uses them to make food for the plant. (A8)

lever (LEHV ur) A simple machine made up of a stiff arm that can move freely around a fixed point. (F91)

life cycle (lyf SY kuhl) The series of changes that a living thing goes through during its lifetime. (A70)

light (lyt) A form of energy that you can see. (F58)

liquid (LIHK wihd) Matter that takes the shape of its container and takes up a definite amount of space. (E7)

magnify (MAG nuh fy) To make an object appear larger. (D38)

mammal (MAM uhl) A vertebrate that has hair or fur, produces milk for its young, and breathes air with its lungs. (A37)

mantle (MAN tl) The thick, middle layer of Earth. (C14)

mass (mas) The amount of matter in an object. (E9)

matter (MAT ur) Anything that has mass and takes up space. (E6)

measure (MEHZ uhr) To use a variety of measuring instruments and tools to find the length, distance, volume, mass, or temperature using appropriate units of measurement.

melt (mehlt) To change state from solid to liquid. (E15)

metamorphic rock (meht uh MAWR fihk rahk) Rock that forms when other rock is changed by heat and pressure. (C18)

mineral (MIHN ur uhl) A material that is found in nature and that has never been alive. (C16)

mixture (MIHKS chur) Matter that is made up of two or more substances or materials that are physically combined. (E35)

moon (moon) A small, rounded body that orbits a planet. (D45)

motion (MOH shuhn) A change in the position of an object. (F72)

natural resource (NACH ur uhl REE sawrs) A material from Earth that is useful to people. (C42)

netted veins (NEHT tihd vaynz) Veins that branch out from main veins. (A16)

new moon (noo moon) The phase of the Moon when the Moon is not visible from Earth because none of its sunlit side faces Earth. (D75)

nonrenewable resource (nahn rih NOO uh buhl REE sawrs) A natural resource that is in limited supply and that cannot be replaced or takes thousands of years to be replaced. (C44)

nutrient (NOO tree uhnt) A substance that living things need in order to survive and grow. (A7)

observe (UHB zuhrv) To use the senses and tools to gather or collect information and determine the properties of objects or events.

offspring (AWF sprihng) The living thing made when an animal reproduces. (A78)

omnivore (AHM nuh vawr) An animal that eats both plants and animals. (B51)

orbit (AWR biht) To move in a path, usually around a planet or a star. (D44)

ore (AWR) Rock that contains metal or other useful minerals. (C42)

organism (AWR guh nihz uhm) Any living thing. (B8)

outer planets (OW tur PLAN ihts) The four planets farthest from the Sun: Jupiter, Saturn, Uranus, and Neptune. (D47)

parallel veins (PAR uh lehl vaynz) Veins that run in straight lines next to each other. (A16)

phases of the Moon (FAYZ ihz uhv thuh moon) The different ways the Moon looks throughout the month. (D76)

physical change (FIHZ ih kuhl chaynj) A change in the size, shape, or state of matter. (E14)

physical property (FIHZ ih kuhl PRAHP ur tee) A characteristic of matter that can be measured or observed with the senses. (E7)

pitch (pihch) How high or low a sound seems. (F18)

planet (PLAN iht) A large body in space that orbits a star. (D44)

plant (plant) A living thing that grows on land or in the water, cannot move from place to place, and usually has green leaves. (A6)

polar climate (POH lur KLY miht) A climate with long, cold winters and short, cool summers. (D27)

pollution (puh LOO shuhn) 1. Any harmful material in the environment. (B34); 2. The addition of harmful materials to the environment. (C60)

population (pahp yuh LAY shuhn) All the organisms of the same kind that live together in an ecosystem. (B14)

potential energy (puh TEHN shuhl EHN ur jee) Stored energy. (F8)

precipitation (prih sihp ih TAY shuhn) Any form of water that falls from clouds to Earth's surface. (D8)

predict (prih DIHKT) To state what you think will happen based on past experience, observations, patterns, and cause-and-effect relationships.

producer (pruh DOO sur) An organism that uses energy from the Sun to make its own food. (B51)

pulley (PUL ee) A simple machine made up of a rope fitted around a fixed wheel. (F93)

pupa (PYOO puh) The third stage of an insect's life cycle, during which it changes into an adult. (A76)

R

record data (rih KAWRD DAY tuh) To write (in tables, charts, journals), draw, audio record, video record, or photograph, to show observations.

recycle (ree SY kuhl) To collect old materials, process them, and use them to make new items. (C62)

reflect (rih FLEHKT) To bounce off. (F60)

refract (rih FRAKT) To bend. (F61)

renewable resource (rih NOO uh buhl REE sawrs) A natural resource that can be replaced by nature. (C44)

reproduce (ree proh DOOS) To make new living things of the same kind. (A26)

reptile (REHP tyl) A vertebrate that has dry, scaly skin and lays eggs on land. (A41)

research (rih SURCH) To learn more about a subject by looking in books, newspapers, magazines, CD-ROMs, searching the Internet, or asking science experts.

resource (REE sawrs) A material found in nature that is useful to organisms. (B15)

revolve (rih VAHLV) To move in a path around an object. (D68)

root (root) The part of a plant that takes in water and nutrients and provides support for the plant. (A8)

rotate (ROH tayt) To turn on an axis. (D68)

S

satellite (SAT l yt) Any object that revolves around a planet or other larger object. (D74)

scientific inquiry (sy uhn TIHF uhk ihn - KWIHR ee) The ways scientists ask and answer questions about the world, including investigating and experimenting. (S4)

screw (skroo) A simple machine made up of an inclined plane wrapped around a column. (F95)

sedimentary rock (sehd uh MEHN tuh ree rahk) Rock that forms when sediment is pressed together and hardens. (C18)

seed (seed) The first stage in the life cycle of most plants. (A70)

simple machine (SIHM puhl muh SHEEN) A tool with few parts that makes work easier. (F90)

soil (soyl) The loose material that covers much of Earth's surface. (C30)

solar energy (SOH lur EHN ur jee) The energy that comes from the Sun and provides Earth with light and heat. (B44)

solar system (SOH lur SIHS tuhm) The Sun and the planets, moons, and other objects that orbit the Sun. (D45)

solid (SAHL ihd) Matter that has a definite shape and takes up a definite amount of space. (E7)

solution (suh LOO shuhn) A special kind of mixture in which two or more substances are so evenly mixed that the separate parts cannot be seen. (E52)

space probe (spays prohb) A craft that explores outer space carrying instruments, but not people. (D58)

speed (speed) A measure of how fast or slow an object is moving. (F84)

star (stahr) A ball of hot gases that gives off light and other forms of energy. (D84)

stem (stehm) The part of a plant that holds up the leaves and carries water and nutrients through the plant. (A8)

substance (SUHB stuhns) A single kind of matter that has certain properties. (E34)

Sun (suhn) The nearest star to Earth. (D44)

tadpole (TAD pohl) The stage in a frog's life cycle when it hatches from the egg and has a long tail, gills, and no legs. (A77)

technology (tek NAHL uh jee) The tools people make and use and the things they build with tools. (S11)

telescope (TEHL ih skohp) A tool that makes distant objects appear larger and sharper. (D38)

temperate climate (TEHM pur iht KLY miht) A climate with warm or hot summers and cool or cold winters. (D26)

temperature (TEHM pur uh chur) The measure of how hot or cold something is. (D16, F50)

terrestrial habitat (tuh REHS tree uhl HAB ih tat) A place where organisms live on land. (B62)

thermal energy (THUR muhl EHN ur jee) The energy of moving particles in matter. (F42)

thermometer (thur MAHM ih tur) A tool that is used to measure temperature. (F50)

tropical climate (TRAHP ih kuhl KLY miht) A climate that is very warm and wet for most of or all of the year. (D26)

trough (trawf) The lowest point of a wave. (F15)

use models (yooz MAHD lz) To use sketches, diagrams or other physical representations of an object, process, or idea to better understand or describe how it works.

use numbers (yooz NUHM burz) To use numerical data to count, measure, estimate, order, and record data to compare objects and events.

use variables (yooz VAIR ee uh buhlz) To keep all conditions in an experiment the same except for the variable, or the condition that is being tested in the experiment.

vein (vayn) A tube that carries food, water, and nutrients throughout a leaf. (A16)

vertebrate (VUR tuh briht) An animal that has a backbone. (A36)

vibrate (VY brayt) To move back and forth quickly. (F16)

volume (VAHL yoom) 1. The amount of space that matter takes up. (E9); 2. How loud or soft a sound seems. (F19)

water cycle (WAH tur SY kuhl) The movement of water between the air and Earth as it changes state. (D8)

water vapor (WAH tur VAY pur) Water in the form of an invisible gas. (D6)

wave (wayv) A movement that carries energy from one place to another. (F14)

weather (WEHTH ur) The condition of the atmosphere at a certain place and time. (D16)

weathering (WEHTH ur ihng) The breaking up or wearing away of rock. (C30)

wedge (wehj) A simple machine made up of two inclined planes. (F95)

wheel and axle (hweel and AK suhl) A simple machine made up of a small cylinder, or axle, attached to the center of a larger wheel. (F92)

work (work) The movement of an object by a force. (F90)

Index

Permission Acknowledgements

Excerpt from Deer, Moose, Elk, and Caribou, by Deborah Hodge, illustrated by Pat Stevens. Text Copyright © 1998 by Deborah Hodge. Illustrations copyright © 1998 by Pat Stevens. Reprinted by permission of Kids Can Press, Ltd., Toronto. Excerpt from The Wump World, by Bill Peet. Copyright © 1970 by Bill Peet. Reprinted by permission of Houghton Mifflin Company. Excerpt from Thunder and Lightning from How & Why Stories: World Tales Kids Can Read & Tell, by Martha Hamilton and Mitch Weiss. Copyright © 1999 Martha Hamilton and Mitch Weiss. Reprinted by permission of Marian Reiner on behalf of August House Publishers, Inc. Excerpt from Thunderstorms What is a Thunderstorm? from Hurricanes Have Eyes But Can't See, by Melvin and Gilda Berger. Copyright © 2003, 2004 by Melvin and Gilda Berger. Reprinted by permission of Scholastic Inc. Excerpt from Freckle Juice, by Judy Blume. Text copyright © 1971 by Judy Blume. Reprinted with the permission of Harold Ober Associates Incorporated and Simon & Schuster Books for Young Readers, an imprint of Simon & Schuster Children's Publishing Division. Excerpt from Freckle Juice, by Judy Blume. Text copyright © 1971 by Judy Blume. Reprinted with the permission of Simon & Schuster Books for Young Readers, an imprint of Simon & Schuster Children's Publishing Division and Harold Ober Associates Incorporated.

Cover

(Toucan) © Steve Bloom/stevebloom.com. (Rainforest bkgd) © Bill Brooks/Masterfile. (Back cover toucan) Masterfile Royalty Free (Spine) Natural Visions/Alamy.

Photography

Unit A Opener: Doug Perrine/Innerspace Visions/Seapics.com. **A1** Michael S. Nolan/AGE Fotostock. **A3** (tr) Burke/Triolo/Brand X/Picturequest. (br) Karl & Kay Amman/Bruce Coleman Inc. (lc) Grant Heilman Photography. **A2–A3** (bkgd) Photo 24/Brand X. **A6–A7** (b) Charles O'Rear/Corbis. (t) Terry W. Eggers/Corbis. **A8** (r) © Phil Degginger/Color Pic, Inc. (c) © Dwight Kuhn. **A9** (r) © Dwight Kuhn. (bc) Microfield Scientific LTD/Science Photo Library/Photo Researchers, Inc. **A10** Melanie Acevedo/Botanica/Getty Images. **A11** (tr) Peter Chadwick/DK Images. (br) Dave King/DK Images. **A10–A11** (b) David M. Schleser/Nature's Images, Inc./Photo Researchers, Inc. **A13** (t) Charles O'Rear/Corbis. (c) © Phil Degginger/Color Pic, Inc. **A14** (bl) Judy White/Garden Photos. **A14–A15** (bkgd) Roger Ressmeyer/Corbis. **A16** (r) Neil Fletcher & Matthew Ward/DK Images. (l) Matthew Ward/DK Images. **A17** (bl) Andrew McRobb/DK Images. (br) Nigel Cattlin/Holt Studios Int./Photo Researchers, Inc. (tl) Norman Owen Tomalin/Bruce Coleman, Inc. (tc) Neil Fletcher & Matthew Ward/DK Images. (tr) Ian O'Leary/DK Images. **A18** (br) © Dwight Kuhn. (tl) ChromaZone Images/Index Stock Imagery. (tr) © E.R. Degginger/Color Pic, Inc. (bl) John Kaprielian/Photo Researchers, Inc. **A19** (t) Matthew Ward/DK Images. (c) ChromaZone Images/Index Stock Imagery. (b) © Dwight Kuhn. **A21** (cr) Dave King/DK Images. **A20–A21** (bkgd) Bruce Dale/National Geographic/Getty Images. **A22** (bl) © E.R. Degginger/Color Pic, Inc. **A22–A23** (bkgd) Natural Selection Stock Photography. **A24** (bl) Francois Gohier/Francois Gohier Nature Photography. (r) Michael & Patricia Fogden/Corbis. **A25** (r) Michael Fogden/DRK Photo. (l) © E.R. Degginger/Color Pic, Inc. **A26** (br) Angelo Cavalli/Superstock. (tl) © Dwight Kuhn. (bl) © Dave Kuhn/Dwight Kuhn Photography. **A27** (c) Michael Fogden/DRK Photo. (t) Michael & Patricia Fogden/Corbis. (b) Angelo Cavalli/Superstock. **A33** (t) A. & S. Carey/Masterfile. (c) Geoff Dann/DK Images. (b) Chip Clark/Smithsonian Museum of Natural History. **A32–A33** (bkgd) Bios/Peter Arnold. **A34** (bl) George Shelley/Masterfile. **A35** (picture card, snake) GK Hart/Vikki Hart/Photodisc/Getty Images. (picture card, bird) GK Hart/Vikki Hart/Photodisc/Getty Images. **A34–A35** (bkgd) Miep Van Damm/Masterfile. **A36** Ernest Janes/Bruce Coleman, Inc. **A37** (t) Tom & Dee Ann McCarthy/Corbis. (b) © E.R. Degginger/Color Pic, Inc. **A38** (c) Mervyn Rees/Alamy Images. (b) Tom Tietz/Stone/Getty Images. (tl) Photri. **A39** (bkgd) Jeff Greenberg/Photo Edit, Inc. **A39** (tr) Jeff Hunter/The Image Bank/Getty Images. (t) Brandon Cole Marine Photography/Alamy Images. (c) Franklin Viola/Animals Animals. **A40** (b) Frank Krahmer/Bruce Coleman, Inc. (tr) Gregory G. Dimijian/Photo Researchers, Inc. **A41** (t) C.K. Lorenz/Photo Researchers, Inc. (b) Sidney Bahrt/Photo Researchers, Inc. (c) Gerry Ellis/Minden Pictures. **A42** (tc) Daniel Zupanc/Bruce Coleman, Inc. (b) Art Wolfe/Getty Images. (c) Jeff Rotman/Photo Researchers, Inc. (t) Art Wolfe/Photo Researchers, Inc. (bc) Corbis. **A44** (bl) Larry West/Bruce Coleman, Inc. **A44–A45** (bkgd) Gary Meszaros/Dembinsky Photo Associates. **A46** (c) I & K Stewart/Bruce Coleman, Inc. (bl) Christy Gavitt/DRK Photo. (br) Jett Britnell/DRK Photo. **A47** (c) Carl Roessler/Bruce Coleman, Inc. (t) Grant

Credits